Love EFT

Positive EFT For Love, Romance & Relationships

1st Paperback Edition

2015

Silvia Hartmann

DragonRising Publishing

United Kingdom

www.DragonRising.com

Love EFT © Silvia Hartmann 2014/2015
ISBN: 978-1-908269-46-1
This is the 1st Paperback Edition: February 14th, 2015
All Rights Reserved In All Media & Languages.

Published By DragonRising Publishing
United Kingdom
www.DragonRising.com

Also by Silvia Hartmann

Energy EFT
Positive EFT
EMO Energy In Motion
Events Psychology
Infinite Creativity

Dedication

To All The Lovers In The World ...

Table of Contents

Positive Energy EFT

Welcome To Love EFT

In this book, you will find the practical applications of the latest discoveries in modern energy work on the most challenging human topic - that of love, romance and human relationships.

Love matters are matters of energy, pure and simple.

Energy is emotion, and if we want to solve our love problems and evolve our love lives in a spectacular way, here is the short cut we have all been searching for.

Loving is easy if you know how ... ☺

Love makes no sense to "the mind" and feels cataclysmic in the "the body" - but its origin is in the energy system and this is where we need to go to move forward in love.

First, we are going to start with a review on how energy works, how it manifests in emotion and our true 6th Sense and learn Positive Energy EFT.

This will take us away from the endless labyrinths of psychotherapy which sought to find non energy based explanations for energy based occurrences and so could not help but fail miserably.

It will takes us off the psychotherapist's couch and back into reality.

Into the reality of our emotions and 6th sense sensations, into the reality of our experiences and most of all, into the amazing reality of what happens when we start treating the energy body right.

This is an exciting journey and we are right here at the beginning.

I welcome you with delight!

Silvia Hartmann
February 14th, 2014

11

Positive EFT

EFT Emotional Freedom Techniques is a wonderfully simple and likewise, immensely profound method to remove blockages to success, health and happiness in our lives and to quite literally, re-energize us so we have the energy, the power, the inspiration we need.

Over the last 15 years, millions of people from all around the world, from all walks of life, old and young alike have found EFT to be a reliable, easy way to help themselves and others with problems of all kinds in a whole new way.

This new way really is a *new way*.

EFT may be using energy points and places that have been talked and written about for at least ten thousand years, but the way in which we apply modern EFT is something that has never been done in the history of humanity before.

In this way, EFT opens the doors to experiences we have never had before and this is tremendously exciting.

When we apply EFT to our problems, not only do the problems go away, but there is more.

We learn that we can become energized; that where there was fear, now there is courage and pride; where there was sadness and grief, now there is the freedom; and where there was anger and hatred, there can be love. There is still more to it - when our emotions change, so do our thoughts and our bodies, as well.

When we feel energized, powerful and happy, our thinking becomes clearer, more logical; we gain access to the powers of our mind. Likewise, when we are energized, our bodies become happier; they feel stronger, healthier, lighter and younger, too.

After all these years and all these experiences, it is still most wonderful to consider that so many good things can come from something as simple as EFT. All we have to do is to remove energy blockages from our energy body, and then go on to improve the flow of energy even further, and we really do become more energized in every sense of the word.

What is also wonderful about EFT and what sets it apart from the ancient forms of emotional control through energy work is that EFT is so personal for each one of us.

Instead of having to think and meditate on "off the peg" ideas or stand in a row to think the same thoughts and do the same movements as everyone else, we get to work with our own individual problems and challenges instead.

We get to choose what we want to treat, what we want to deal with; we get to have our say what we want out of life at last. Each one of us is highly individual.

We were born all different to start with, and then our life experiences went on to shape us, make us more and more different with each day that passed, with each experience - good and bad alike - that was had. So it stands to reason that each one of us has our own challenges, and our own order and sequence in which to approach these challenges as we go through life.

For some, EFT can help with health; for others, relationships are the most important issue. Someone else might want to address memories that haunt them first of all, and others may have life long problems with stress, addictions, low self esteem, sadness, grief or anger.

- **EFT allows us to direct its effects wherever we want to start, and whatever we want to apply it to.**

This is truly revolutionary and it is also what makes EFT so immensely effective.

Further, we don't have to wait around for the next "sacred circle time" of therapy or healing with EFT.

We can use EFT at any time, anywhere we go; and therefore, we can treat the daily upsets and the "stuff" that happens on an ongoing basis, again highly personalised, as and when we need it.

EFT is quite literally in your own hands.

Once you have learned the simple protocol, you own it; it is yours and it is yours to use, any time, anywhere. There are no expensive machines involved; there are no repeat prescriptions. EFT is yours to use forever, and freely share with others too, and all it takes is ten minutes to show someone what to do and where the treatment points are.

What a wonderful gift - we can hardly begin to appreciate this completely.

If you are new to EFT, we can also tell you that it gets better and better with practice and experience.

Even though EFT can help you feel better right away, especially if you don't stop too soon and keep tapping until you feel really energized (this is a core part of EFT Energy!), this is still only the beginning.

When we apply EFT, we quite practically step into a whole new world of possibilities and potential, far beyond the mere symptom cessation we currently crave.

In this book you will find the Energy EFT Protocol, all the instructions and exercises you need to get started with Positive EFT.

The most important piece of advice at the beginning is:

- **Simply start tapping positives!**

EFT works with real people who live in the real world, today, in the 21st Century. These are very different people to those who lived 6,000 years ago; we have challenges and experiences those who devised the ancient ways of working with energy could not have foreseen in their wildest dreams. We eat differently, act differently, think very differently and the range of problems we face on a daily basis were completely unknown back in the day when people lived in little villages, worked on farms and had their life's paths mapped out from the cradle to the grave, reliably.

Even if you had no luck with some of the older methods around, take heart and give Positive EFT a fresh start.

Allow yourself to become fascinated by the EFT protocol, how it feels and how it affects you.

Pay attention even to small sensations, shifts and movements in your thoughts, body sensations and emotions - you are learning not just EFT, but important new things about yourself, how you work, how mind/body/spirit interact and influence each other in your own particular and absolutely unique case.

There are many wonderful aspects to the practice of Positive EFT; that we start understand ourselves better and as a result, gain a better relationship with ourselves in the process is high on the list of benefits.

In this spirit, be gentle with yourself; follow the simple instructions, pay attention to your own stress levels and start by treating stress first of all so you are in a calm and curious state of mind when you start your own exploration of Positive EFT and now, let us no longer delay and find out more about Positive EFT, how it works, and how you can make it work for you.

How Positive EFT Works

<u>**All**</u> human beings have an *energy body*.

What exactly one particular person's energy body is like, we do not know as we can't see or measure the energy body.

There are some basic things we can know about the energy body:

The energy body has a head of energy, the energy mind.

The energy body has hands made from energy, the healing hands.

The energy body has energy organs such as the *heart centre.*

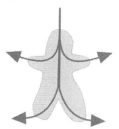

The energy body has many energy flows and *energy channels* that transport energy in, through and out of itself.

ENERGY MUST FLOW

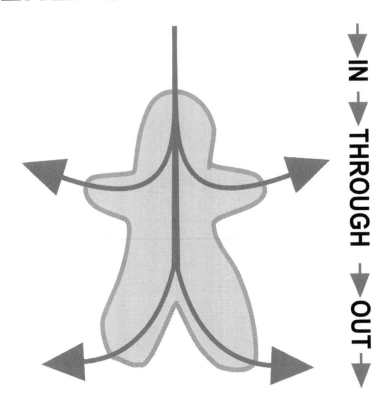

In order to function properly, ***energy must flow*** freely **into** the energy body, **through** and **out**.

Sometimes, the flow of energy becomes blocked.

When this happens, problems arise in the energy body:

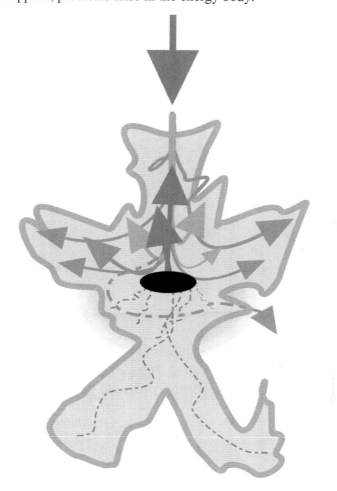

Please note how the blockage doesn't just affect the direct erea[1] of where it is located, but how all the energy flows are being disturbed and disrupted because of it. Energy blockages have all sorts of side effects and really throw the mind/body/energy body system out of balance.

If this energy blockage was removed, it is easy to understand how this person would feel much better - from relief at the top to having more energy at the bottom, and feel more "right" in themselves, and definitely more alive, more "energized."

---

1 erea - Short for "existing energetic reality."

In EFT, we tap on certain energy points to improve the flow of energy and clear the blockages.

When the blockages are cleared, a person starts to feel different, better and more energized.

Emotions change, thoughts change, and many other things change as a result.

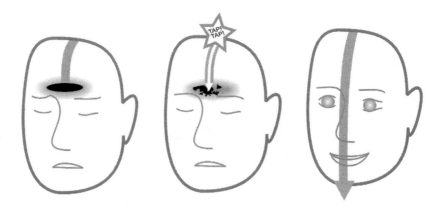

EFT Works By Increasing The Flow Of Energy Through The Energy Body.

When there is positive, powerful flow of energy through the energy body, we experience **positive emotions** - happiness, personal power, feeling good, feeling compassionate, feeling loving.

When the flow of energy in the energy system is disrupted, we feel **negative emotions** instead - stress, panic, anger, sadness and all the many different ways the real feelings in the physical body that are our emotions have been labelled.

- **When we tap on the energy points to improve energy flow in the energy body, we can unlock energy blockages.**

Energy flow improves, and we start to feel better. We tap some more to improve the energy flow even further - and we get to feel even better still! It is that simple, and because it is simple and true, EFT works so well and has helped so many people overcome so many problems.

Thereby, instead of trying to undo the thoughts or memories in some way, which has been attempted by millions in therapy for many years and with highly unpredictable results, by working with EFT at the real source of the problem, with the energy body, we finally have a real tool to "make us feel better" - for the first time in recorded human history.

As you will see, this simple yet profound discovery doesn't only make perfect sense, it has also proven itself in practice - there are now tens of thousands of therapists all across the world, daily relieving clients of all kinds of long standing problems using variations on this idea, successfully, predictably, time and time again. And just as importantly, there are many, many more individual people who are using EFT to help themselves feel better all around the world today.

Theory and conscious understanding is all good and well, but you don't really begin to appreciate the truth of how amazing and wonderful Positive EFT is - until you have experienced it for yourself.

In a moment, we're going to learn how to do Positive EFT, and you can pick any positive energy form and try it out for yourself.

What Can We Gain With Positive EFT?

Positive EFT is not a "miracle" - although it really feels that way!

Positive EFT works simply by improving the flow of energy through the energy body. This gives us a very different perspective and a different way to get what we want out of life.

When energy flow becomes higher, emotional, mental and physical experience begin to change. Most of all, we begin to feel better - we begin to experience POSITIVE EMOTIONS.

Emotions are the feedback devices that tell us about the conditions in the energy body.

- **Negative emotions are caused by LOW ENERGY - disturbances and blockages in the energy body, making us "feel bad."**

- **Positive emotions are caused by HIGH ENERGY - the energy body flowing freely, powerfully and that makes us "feel good."**

- **There is no good and bad energy - only energy, and the absence of energy.**

Real emotions have a physical component. This means you can physically feel sensations of trembling, pressure, heat, churning, pounding, fluttering and so on in your physical body. These are messages from the energy body, transmitted through the physical body so we can do something about them, just the same as stepping on a rusty nail would hurt in the physical foot.

Energy body stress is the big spanner in the works of humanity today.

As so little was known about energy and emotions, people in the past didn't understand the connection between emotions and movements in the energy body. With EFT, we can reliably and predictably improve energy flow and that will cause us to "feel better" in the literal sense of the word.

- **Treating emotional disturbances, emotional stress and emotional pain is the first and most important application of EFT.**

Many if not all human problems have some form of stress disturbance attached to them.

For example, when someone gets physically sick, they can also become scared and unhappy.

When we work with EFT to improve their emotions about being sick, and we improve the flow of energy through their energy body, we might not be healing their sickness, but we will make them feel better.

We will also release a lot of emotional stress from the whole person, so the body stands a better chance of repairing itself more quickly.

- **Positive EFT does not treat physical illness.**

EFT can only treat the energy system components of a problem; but in doing so, many positive effects can happen.

- **Likewise, EFT does not treat physical pain.**

However, physical pain often has an energy or emotional component to it; when we release this with EFT, the experience of pain changes. This can lead to pain reduction, or the pain being experienced differently; we can't say in advance how the application of EFT will affect any one person.

We can certainly say that it is worth **trying Positive EFT on *everything*.**

When the energy body is strong and happy, any challenge becomes so much easier.

Positive EFT is not a miracle cure to heal all ills of mankind, but a sensible, powerful intervention to help people who are stressed to become stronger in body, clearer in mind, and to experience empowering, positive emotions.

Positive EFT is quick, it feels wonderful and improving the flow of energy through the energy body is always a good thing to do, so we say:

"Try Positive EFT On Everything!"

How To Do Positive EFT

Tapping EFT

The EFT treatment points are stimulated by tapping lightly on them.

Even though we are using our physical hands on our physical body, we are not trying to massage muscles, bones or tissue but instead **it is our energy hands tapping on our energy body** which produce the results.

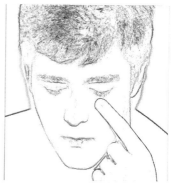

- **Each individual tap is like closing an electric circuit.**

As such, tapping "harder" doesn't do the trick; but tapping with awareness and paying attention to the contact between your fingertip and your body as you tap really helps.

You can tap with either hand on either side of the bilateral points. Normally people will tap with the index finger of their leading hand on the opposite side of the face. You can choose either side on the bilateral points.

Try now tapping the point under your eye, with your index finger, quite gently and rhythmically, as many times as it takes for you to take a normal breath in and out.

The strength of tapping should be light, just enough so that you feel a resonance from the tapping spreading out across a reasonable part of that side of your face when you pay close attention.

Different people have different speeds of tapping, and the speed of tapping often relates naturally to what we are tapping on. We generally show a tapping speed in the rhythm of "Jingle Bells."

The EFT diagram is on the next page.

Start with the Heart Position and tap all the points from the Top Of The Head to the Karate Chop point, ending up with the Heart Position at the end. Have a go right now to get the feel of doing EFT.

Remember to breathe deeply throughout and move towards finding a rhythm between the tapping and your breath so that the EFT round flows easily and smoothly all the way from the beginning to the end.

- **A single EFT round is from Heart Position to Heart Position, with all the points from the Top of the Head to the Karate Chop point in between.**

Energy EFT Tapping Chart

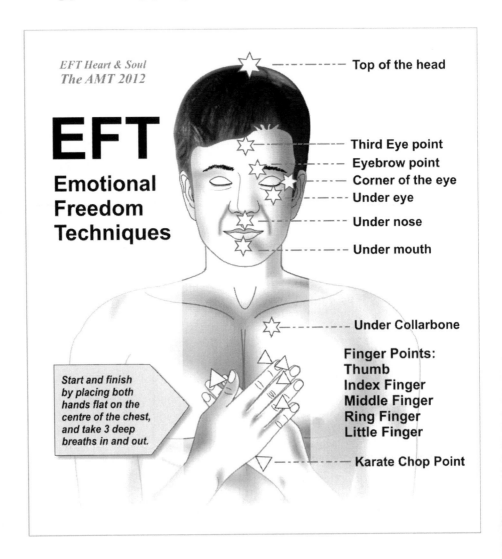

The EFT Round

EFT uses major energy centres and special energy points or meridian points to stimulate and improve the flow of energy through the energy body.

0 = **The Heart Centre**. This is where we start and finish our round of EFT by placing both hands flat on the centre of the chest in the Heart Position and take three deep breaths in and out.

1. **Top Of The Head** - The highest point on the top of your head.
2. **Third Eye Point** - In the centre of your forehead.
3. **Start Of The Eyebrow** - Where the bone behind your eyebrow turns into the bridge of your nose.
4. **Corner Of The Eye** - On the bone in the corner of your eye.
5. **Under The Eye** - On the bone just below your eye, in line with your pupil if you look straight ahead.
6. **Under The Nose** - Between you nose and your upper lip
7. **Under The Mouth** - In the indentation between your chin and your lower lip
8. **Under The Collarbone** - In the angle formed by your collarbone and the breastbone
9. **Thumb** - all finger points are on the side of the finger, in line with the nail bed.
10. **Index Finger**
11. **Middle Finger**
12. **Ring Finger**
13. **Little Finger**
14. **Karate Chop Point** - on the side of your hand, roughly in line with your life line.

0 = And to finish the round of EFT, back to the **Heart Position** where we take three deep breaths in and out.

Take a moment now go through the sequence, starting with the Heart Position where you take three deep breaths in and out. Then find and touch each point in turn with your index finger.

Touch each point lightly, breathe deeply and simply pay attention to how that feels, and how each point creates all kinds of different sensations you can feel in your body.

The Energy Body Stress Factor

The higher the energy flow in the energy body, the "better" **ANY** person becomes.

The energy body stress table shows us that any person becomes "a better person" when there is more energy flowing through their energy body.

This improvement is measurable in mental performance, physical performance and in emotional stability.

- **Any human being at all, regardless how old, young, what their gender may be, their previous experiences or current level of health, will improve across the board in mind, body and spirit when energy flow is increased.**

Conversely, any human being becomes a worse human being when they are stressed.

This has very powerful repercussions for a person's self concept.

It finally explains how someone can be sequentially nice and nasty, friendly and antisocial, intelligent and stupid, capable and useless - how well we perform at anything is dependent on our energy body stress levels.

To understand this also transforms how we understand other people, and how we deal with them.

To understand that a stressed person is just stressed (rather than "mad, bad and dangerous" or "born bad") allows us to treat them differently, to use very different strategies to help them and bring them back to better states of functioning.

This is of the utmost importance in dealing with children but also with adults, both in private contexts as well as in professional and business relationships.

The Energy Chart

-10 So much stress damage that the system shuts down and does not restore itself (catatonia)

-9 Extremely high stress causes temporary shut down (fit, panic attack followed by fainting)

- 8 Very high stress causes extremely severe disturbances (self mutilation, autism, blind rage, "going berserk," "madness")

- 7 Very high stress causing extreme disturbances (extreme temper tantrums, self abuse, schizophrenic metaphors, uncontrollable memory flashes, "crazy ideas")

- 6 High stress causing high disturbances (temper tantrums, high end addictions, illogical thinking, immediate gratification, unstable, highly egocentric)

- 5 Full stress (irritability, inability to concentrate, not in control of thoughts & memories, communication failure, inability to enter rapport, social, mental and physical malfunctioning)

- 4 General stress (lapses in ability to control thoughts, emotions and behaviour, lack of long term planning ability, overexcited, stubborn, closed mind, impaired communication skills)

- 3 Medium stress (talking, thinking and moving a too fast, trying to do too much, putting in more effort than the situation requires, lack of empathy)

- 2 Low Stress (slight impairment in emotional control, not entirely "clear" on future goals and current situations, slight impairment in social skills)

- 1 Very low stress (occasional infrequent flashes of uninvited thoughts)

0 No stress (calm, tranquil, peaceful, no action required, resting, relaxing, sleepy)

+ 1 Very low energy flow (neutral, aware, occasional flashes of positive thoughts & emotions)

+ 2 Low energy flow (vague sense of potential, hope, feeling like "waking up from a sleep")

+ 3 Medium energy flow (feeling ok, smiling, beginning to move, enjoying the present)

+ 4 Improving energy flow (breathing deeply, increased body awareness, more movement, feeling good, starting to think about the future, able and willing to communicate freely)

+ 5 General energy flow (feeling wide awake, happy, ready for action, wanting to take action, wanting to interact and communicate)

+ 6 Faster energy flow (feeling exciting physical sensations, more expansive thinking, feeling personally powerful, feeling excited, enjoying communication, high social awareness)

+ 7 Very fast energy flow (re-thinking and re-organising concepts, expanded awareness, feeling powerful positive emotions, feeling alive, feeling love)

+ 8 High energy flow (picking up personal power, feeling delighted, making new decisions, very fast and very logical thinking, high social abilities: networking, rapport and communication)

+ 9 Very high energy flow (delighted, tingling all over, very excited, joyful, actively loving)

+ 10 Optimal energy flow (enlightenment experience, unconditional love)

The Scurvy Story

A long time ago, when sailing ships first started to cross oceans, there was a disease called "scurvy" which would affect the sailors.

Their hair and teeth would fall out; they would become emotionally unstable, physically clumsy, and suffer from a variety of other symptoms, including sleep disturbances, skin rashes, ear and eye infections, digestive problems and mental impairment.

Each different symptom was being treated in exclusion, to little effect; finally, someone had the bright idea to include Vitamin C which had been lacking in their diets.

Just a few drops of lime juice each day, and the sailors regained their health.

People in our modern age have no idea where all their stress is coming from; and modern medicine is treating all the various stress related problems in exclusion, one at a time, one pill per symptom, as it were.

When a person's energy body gets low on energy, symptoms multiply and they get worse and worse, the lower the energy flow becomes.

This causes disturbances across the board, making people physically, mentally and emotionally appear to be beset by mystery illnesses of all kinds.

We need to improve the energy body's diet; we need to give it positive, nourishing energy forms so it begins to function again.

When that happens, a whole host of symptoms and problems disappear as if by magic.

The problems that do not disappear are then real problems, which can be treated appropriately and in the correct way.

Feeding the energy body correctly costs nothing at all, it is interesting, feels good and makes people happier - we have nothing to lose, and so very much to gain!

Living Life With A Full Battery

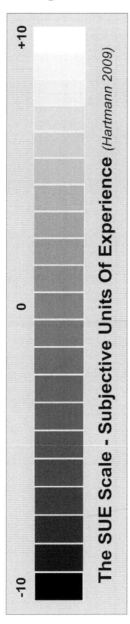

The SUE Scale - Subjective Units Of Experience *(Hartmann 2009)*

There are all sorts of things modern human beings do which disturb the energy system.

The more stressed the energy system becomes, the worse we feel ...

... about ourselves

... about other people

... about the whole world.

Life becomes hard and painful.

It gets worse as energy flow becomes more and more disrupted.

- **Low energy flow leads to disturbed emotions, disturbed thinking and makes the body weak as well.**

When energy flow is low, we try to live life with a depleted battery.

We simply don't have the strength to do the work we need to do and we don't have much left to give to others.

We need to learn to quite literally re-charge the batteries of our energy systems - and to do that, we need positive energy forms that empower the energy system and bring it back to life.

Positive energy feeds the energy body and re-charges your batteries of life.

High Energy Flow

The energy system works best when it is in full flow - *at least* +5 on the energy scale.

This is a state similar to when you are in love.

Gravity is lighter, the colours are brighter, you feel strong, young, powerful and happy in every fibre of your being, wide awake, and you are kind to everyone.

To move into these high energy states, we need POSITIVE energy forms.

Positive energy forms lift our state (of mind, body and spirit!) higher and make us feel glad to be alive.

We become more powerful, but most importantly, more joyful.

This gives us real strength and the energy we need to create the lives we want to lead.

Tapping Positives

Mind, body and spirit are supposed to work together, all three doing the same thing at the same time.

When we tap EFT on positives,

- we focus the mind by speaking the word/s,
- we engage the body by touching physically,
- and we are stimulating the energy body.

The more attractive the positive energy is to you, the easier it is to get good results.

Overleaf is a list of positives you can choose from to get you started.

1. Choose something you really want in your life.

2. Put both hands on your chest in the Heart Position, take three deep breaths and say the name of the positive energy out aloud.

3. Then lightly tap all of the special energy points, starting from the top of the head. On each point, say the name of the positive loudly and clearly as you tap. Take a deep breath in and out, then move on to the next point.

4. Finish in the Heart Position and take three deep breaths.

Choose a first positive and try this out for yourself now.

Positive Energy Forms For Love & Relationships

Love	Youth	Sparkle	Colour
Wisdom	Wealth	Magic	Lightning
Logic	Play	Creativity	Luck
Wonder	Power	Passion	Strength
Peace	Mystery	Stillness	Sunshine
Bliss	Pride	Tranquillity	Ecstasy
Confidence	Serenity	Union	Freedom
Excitement	Blessings	Rhythm	Harmony
Hope	Vision	Completion	Beauty
Warmth	Evolution	Space	Success
Purpose	Satisfaction	Surprise	Empathy
Clarity	Resonance	Sex	Time
Lifting	Transformation	Energy	Lightness
Kindness	Tenderness	Inspiration	Treasures
Abundance	Immortality	Joy	Truth
Happiness	Stability	Fortune	Vitality
Dance	Togetherness	Gold	Gratitude
Faith	Certainty	Radiance	Connection
Laughter	Respect	Easy	Soul
Miracle	Energy	Respect	Luck
Brilliance	Belonging	Expansion	Trust
Desire	Sensuality	Openness	Awareness
Potential	Delight	Feeling	Fire
Patience	Expansion	Expectation	Celebration
Blessings	Support	Attention	Protection

Even MORE Energy ...

You can tell when energy flow becomes higher when ...

- You start to feel tingling in your body
- You feel lighter, happier, stronger
- You start to relax, move more freely
- You start to breathe more freely and more deeply
- You smile or laugh.

Now, we can tap another round of Energy EFT on the same positive energy form to increase energy flow further.

Use the same positive for the next round and simply add MORE.

So this time, we do the round of EFT from the Heart Position through to the Heart Position at the end and as we tap, we say ...

MORE Joy!

... if Joy was the positive of your choice.

Allow yourself to really, really want more (...) in your life, right now.

This creates a powerful energy movement you can really FEEL in your body - and it feels GOOD!

We were born to feel good.

We are designed to FEEL GOOD.

We are not taking anything away from anyone else, because it's only energy so don't be shy!

Do another round of Energy EFT straight after and allow yourself to invite:

EVEN MORE JOY!!!

And one more round - it only takes about two minutes for each one! and we can tap for ...

ALL THE JOY IN THE UNIVERSE!!!

Fantastic!

Using The SUE Scale To Measure Energy Flow

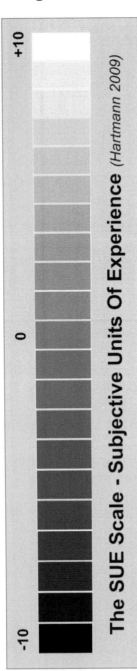

The SUE Scale helps us measure how stressed or energized we are.

We can use it to notice how stressed we are, and when we are tapping the positives, how much progress we have made towards the perfect 10, which is the best you can feel at this time.

This can be useful, because we are not used to feeling really good, really on top form very often.

There is so much personal, professional and global stress around, often people are not seeing the wood for the trees and don't even realise just how stressed they have been, and for how long.

Try this for yourself. First, pick a positive or think of something you really want in your life right now, let's say SUCCESS.

You can look at the SUE scale, put your finger on it, and ask yourself, "How much success do I have in my life already?"

This gives us a starting point, and it really does not matter if that starting point is at -8 or at +5 because we want SUCCESS, then MORE SUCCESS, and then ALL THE SUCCESS IN THE UNIVERSE!!!

We are working with energy and feelings in the body, feeding your energy body and making it strong.

After each round of EFT, you can check the SUE scale.

Keep going until you reach the perfect +10 and you feel great, alive - and ready for SUCCESS!

Tips On Tapping Positive EFT

1. Allow Yourself To Really WANT Positive Energy In Your Life!

When you pick a positive, take a moment to allow yourself to really, REALLY want it.

The more "hungry" you can allow yourself to be, the more of a tidal draw you create in your energy system, and the more energy can flow into you as a direct result.

It is important to understand that you don't need to know how more (luck, joy, sex, wealth, power, respect etc. etc.) is going to come into your life as a result of what you are doing here.

It also doesn't matter at all if you think you deserve it or not, and you don't even have to know exactly what that "means" - all you have to do from your end is to WANT IT.

We want these things which money can't buy; they are energy forms which create emotions and sensations we can feel, and which make us feel good.

It is right and natural to fill the wants and needs of your particular energy body, just as it is right and natural to drink water when you are thirsty, or eat something when you are hungry.

The more we feed our energy bodies with the kinds of energies they have hungered for all their lives, the better we feel.

Nature rewards us for doing the right thing! at last. We all have been taught that it is bad to want things, that we should make due or learn to go without; when we work with Positive EFT, we need to let go of that and allow ourselves to want these positive things with the same intensity a small child would have who wants a particular toy.

This is an important part of working with Positive EFT and a wonderful side effect - we become much clearer on what we want in our lives, and that makes it much easier to get many other things too, including material changes we might have sought but which always seemed so out of reach.

2. It's Only Real If You Can Feel It's Real!

Working with Positive EFT is NOT "positive thinking."

Positive thinking doesn't work when your energy system is stressed and miserable. In fact, it can make us feel even worse.

Tapping EFT on a positive is a very different experience.

As we tap and say, "I want ENERGY!" we are simply speaking the truth; and as energy begins to flow more freely, we can really feel the effects.

Pay attention to:

Tingling sensations in your body - those are often the first indications that energy flow is starting up.

Shivers and other sensations that make you want to move (your neck, your shoulders, your feet, your back) - it's important to stay loose and go with those sensations, that helps energy flow much better.

Yawning, tearing of the eyes, waves of strange sensations - that happens when energy blockages start to dissolve and are all natural reactions to improving the energy flow.

Floaty feelings, feeling very relaxed, sleepy - that's what happens around the 0 point on the SUE scale, and it's a sign you are coming up from a stressed state towards better energy flow. It's very important to keep on tapping, you're on the right path!

It's the sensations, the feelings in your body, which are the most important. That's what is telling you something is changing. This is your sixth sense at work, and it is the direct body sensations that tell us, "Yes, you really have an energy body, and yes, something amazing is happening!"

If you don't feel anything much on your first round, don't despair. Many people, and especially men, have been trained to ignore their sixth sense and "not feel emotions."

It takes a while to re-direct your attention to your body sensations.

And it gets better and stronger with practise, so choose another positive and do some more Positive EFT.

3. Loosen Up For Maximum Energy Flow

This is important: The more you can loosen up your body, the faster your energy flow will increase and the better you feel.

Don't screw up your eyes in furious concentration; instead, breathe deeply, relax your shoulders, and MOVE with the sensations that the tapping produces in your body.

Tapping whilst standing up helps a lot.

Opening a window for some fresh air is a good idea.

Shaking out your hands and feet in between rounds, rotating your neck and loosening up your ankles, knees, hips and spine really helps with energy flow too.

When the energy flow becomes fast and high, it is natural to be dancing around the room - that's a good sign you're getting this right.

4. It's Really OK To Feel Good!

Whoever you are and whatever you do, it really is OK for you to feel good. To feel even better, and more often.

The Great Creative Order designed us that way.

The more often you can feel on top of the world, the more stress you are releasing at the same time, and the better your life is going to start to work for you, in every department.

Being happy doesn't make you silly, or irresponsible, or weak - just the opposite.

In order to be the best person we can possibly be, we need to feel happy and strong inside as often as possible. We need to fill our lives with GOOD experiences, good feelings and then we have something to give to others as well.

So please say YES to joy, and luck, and love and all the many other positives that money can't buy - but we can experience thanks to Positive EFT.

Discovering Positive EFT - In Brief

- We have energy bodies which have been neglected.

- Stressed energy bodies lead to negative emotions, thought, behaviour and will eventually also affect health.

- To reverse energy body stress, we need positive energy forms which feed the energy system and make it stronger.

- We can know what kinds of energy forms we need because we can feel what we need.

- Money can't buy the feelings of joy, respect, luck and all the other energy forms - but we HUNGER for them.

- Tapping Positive EFT is a quick and easy way to improve energy flow and start to feel much, much better.

- The more often we can feel better, the more we reduce overall energy body stress and the more effortless and successful life becomes.

- If you can allow yourself a positive energy experience as often as you brush your teeth, your life will transform within the year - guaranteed.

- With practice, evoking and experiencing positive energy forms gets faster, better, and easier.

Love & Energy

Everybody's Looking For Love ...

What do people need?

What are people looking for in life?

What is everybody looking for?

Everybody knows that everybody is looking for love, but not everybody knows yet how to get love. How to get love easily actually and reliably and logically and in such a way that it's inevitable.

Yet it is really, really simple.

Love is and love has been such a problem to humanity primarily because they could never understand the energy system correctly or what the energy system was.

- **Love is an energy system phenomenon.**

Love is something that ignites the energy system to the point where it becomes a physical sensation in the body; then it becomes overwhelming and really changes the person who experiences that. Of course you can't explain that with flesh and bone, and hard theories in a clockwork, mechanical universe.

We are energists. We know we have energy bodies, and knowing this makes the game of love actually remarkably easy.

You could say that it makes it child's play, it is that easy.

So let's just simply start at the beginning and at the beginning we have the energy flow chart.

The energy flow tells us that when we have low energy flow in the energy body, we become more and more miserable and essentially unlovable, unattractive.

People do not want to be around people who are annoying or angry, or negative or stressed, or whining, waling and being miserable. They certainly don't want to be around people who are crazy and insane.

In fact there is an absolute direct cause and effect relationship between how low you are on the energy flow chart, and how unattractive or even repellent other people perceive you to be.

We also have the opposite effect on the other side of the energy chart, where there is positive energy flow, where we're getting into a good energy body state.

- **The higher you get up on the Sue scale or on the energy chart, the more powerfully attractive you become.**

The more your X Factor kicks in, that mysterious something that transcends your age, your race, how fit you are, how many limbs in working order you own, how beautiful you are physically, that X Factor, what love and falling in love is all about.

In this simple realisation we really have the answer to our love and relationship problems which is so simple and so profound at the same time.

It is exactly what the prophets of the ages have always told us. It tallies with our own personal experience, and that of the experience of humanity across the ages, and it is so simple it could not be any simpler.

All we have to do to get more love into our lives is to improve the energy flow through our energy body.

We need to come out of these negative stress states where we are people that we ourselves wouldn't date, or want to be in a relationship with and you know exactly what I am talking about. These negative, low energy states when you are being miserable and whining and bitching, and angry and unhappy, and stomping your feet and shouting abuse at people.

You know we all have these moments, of course we do - and this brings me to a really important understanding.

The Self Concept Buster

We have to start with ourselves here and that's the self concept.

The self concept is when we take all the various things that we've been and done over all the years that we can remember and we put it together in this big ball of madness, which contains being a saint sometimes, being an amazing person with a great capacity to love - and then at other times, just appalling behaviours of lying, cheating and stealing, or being really not the kind of person you would want to be.

This causes people to have this really bizarre mental movement which asks this question, "Who am I? Am I nice or am I nasty? Am I a beautiful soul or am I terrible demon from the very pits of hell?"

Again, our energy chart explains why that is so.

Every person in the world becomes a demon from hell when they get stressed in life.

Just as every person becomes a lovable angel or even beyond when they're filled with energy.

Your X Factor Rating

How lovable you are and what kinds of people you attract, what kind of experiences in love you can expect to attract is directly related to the kind of energy states you find yourself in most commonly.

Now a lot of people have had quite significant damage in their energy system, in the systems that relate to relating to others.

The basic social systems of exchanging energy with other people are damaged, broken, sometimes they got frozen in a very juvenile state, and the symptoms of that just get worse as the person gets older and they get ever more out of sync with societies expectations of a grown man or a grown woman and that is a problem

We do not relate as naturally to each other as we were designed to, that is a fact. There are all sorts of systems that are not working as they should.

There are so many different systems, depending on your life, that are all not working as they should and every single person has their own story, their own problems, their own moments of trauma and freak out, their own times when they needed love and they weren't given it properly.

Every person has their own set of these to the point that you know we could be laying on a psychotherapists couch forever and ever and ever, each one of us and we would never even get to tell the whole story - because to tell the whole story you would have to literally relive every second of your life. That is not a good choice. it's not a good option, and of course by focusing on all the bad things of the past, there is a really big danger of reliving the past and bringing the past into the now rather than thinking about the future.

So what I would like us to do here in this project is to first of all, is to take a deep breath and to say,

"Okay, so it doesn't matter what happened to me in the past, not anymore.

"This is about the now and then about the future.

"I want to have amazing experiences of love, romance, connectedness, in mind, body and spirit. I want to feel feelings, not the old feelings again that I might have had when I was a teenager but I want to feel new feelings, new amazing sensations that I have never felt before yet I know they exist.

"I have this capacity. I have this hunger. I want to have these new experiences, these more amazing experiences of love, sex, and romance!

"This is my desire."

The theory is simple.

If you want to get better at love, you need to get higher up on our light scale here, on our scale of love, our energy scale, to bring our X Factor up so that we become radiant and shiny. That makes us more attractive to others, literally attracting people to you like moths come streaming to the flame and they can't help themselves because they want some of that energy. They need that energy for themselves, to nourish themselves, to heal themselves, so that they may grow up and evolve.

This love energy is what everyone hungers for but it's not just that it makes you immeasurably more attractive.

When you go higher up on the energy chart, your awareness expands. You feel safer, stronger, more grounded and more centred in yourself.

You become far more powerful, and you attract different types of people. The bullies and abusers are on the lookout for victims, not for strong, powerful people, so there is safety built in as well.

You have more access to more information through all your senses, all your senses are heightened and more acute. This brings you more information but also opens the door for these new experiences. These new sensations, these new shivers that will rush through you and make you tingle in places you might never have tingled before.

So this is what this book is all about.

It is about you, it is about the future, it is about new experiences and sensations that you have never had before.

This is about being able to give more love, a better quality kind of love, cleaner, clearer love, because the higher up you go on the energy scale, the more unconditional the expression of your love becomes.

And finally, this is about using the power of love to evolve ourselves and others because it is the love of other people that had this enormous power to wash away all the sins of the past and to give you a different reality, a different experience, brand new experiences from which new lives, new concepts and a whole new you can emerge.

Negative Thoughts

There is a direct correlation between what you think about yourself, or what you feel to be true about yourself, and where you are on the energy scale.

Everybody who's low down on energy feels that they are too ugly, too old, their nose is too big, they might be the wrong race or generation, too stupid, too smart, too this, that and the other.

It really doesn't matter if the main reason why you've never found love is because nobody loved you as a child or because you're black, or because you're a lesbian, or because you're fat, or because you're thin, or because you're too short, or too tall, or one leg is shorter than the other, or your hair is the wrong colour, or it's too curly or too straight.

Negative thoughts are only indicators of low energy states.

The first thing we need to learn here is that all of these kind of thoughts are nothing but an indication how your energy levels are at the time, and I want you to test this out yourself with your own memories.

Remember a time when you were really on form, on song, when you were really "up" and you felt powerful, did you for one moment even think about what your hair looked like on that day? Or whether you were too fat or too thin?

Perhaps you can remember further back, when you were a child and before you learned all these things about you and all these weird things happened that caused your energy system to go down and become reversed and blocked and shattered.

Remember when you were a child running around and you got home and you were full of excitement and it was then the parents pointed out that your hands were dirty or your shoes were dirty or you had a hole in your trousers. Yet you never noticed that at all because you were so involved and engaged in the games you were playing and the experiences you were having.

When your energy system is running well and it is high, and flying high, where were all these negative inward pointing thoughts of "I wonder if I've got the right handbag? I wonder if my shoes match my trousers ... Does my butt look fat in this?"

All of that isn't there; you don't have to defeat it. You don't have to tuck it away, it just can't exist there. These thoughts are like slimy creatures that lurk in the depth and if you bring them up to the surface, they just explode and cease to exist at all. They can't live in real reality, in an energy filled universe where everything is light and dances.

So the first thing that I want us to clearly understand is that negative thoughts about yourself are only indicators of low energy, that is all they are.

Nothing more.

So someone might raise their hand and say, "But it's the truth that my nose is too big to ever find love." It doesn't matter. If you bring raise your energy system up to the positive side on the energy scale, past +3 and beyond, what you will find is that you change your mind.

Your mind changes automatically as you go up on the energy scale.

Instead of saying, "My nose is too big to ever find love," you will find that, "My nose might be big, but I also have got a good heart and so much love to give!"

And as you go even higher still, it becomes simply, "I have so much love to give!"

It goes even higher still and you are left with nothing but, "I am love."

That is the most attractive and wonderful thing to be. When you even get close to that state, people will start noticing you - and become deeply and powerfully attracted to you.

A person who is emanating love is a miracle and highly, highly desirable.

Working with positive energy, we use negative thoughts about ourselves, about our partners and about our relationships as the indicator that we need to ***do something.***

We need to improve our energy flow, immediately, before we think further foolish thoughts. It is important to understand that negative, judgemental, criticising thoughts really are only foolish thoughts.

There is no important truth here, there's no reality to any of that. There is no merit to any of that negative stress thinking that will turn a genius into a fool. It can't help you. Just ask all the people who thought they could make their lives such a different place by having plastic surgery, bigger breasts, or their nose straightened out.

48

At the top level, people who don't look any further than the physical found them pretty all of a sudden when they didn't before, but where's the love? And how does that person feel inside who now has a plastic nose? Do they feel any more beautiful? Do they feel any more powerful? Or do they simply have to find something else they can now blame because they can't blame the nose any longer for the lack of love in their lives?

So now, if we look back at our energy chart for a moment, all that needs to be done in order to have a better self concept, better self esteem, and better access to the facilities that protect us, that guide us, give us good ideas and tell us what we need to do next, in order to make happen what we want to happen and make us happy - all these things simply require that we bring our energy levels up.

One approach, and the benefits are inconceivable.

Raise your energy levels to be the best person you can be.

Now how do we do that? Well there are lots of different methods available these days to raise energy fast, and the most famous one probably at this point is EFT.

We can tap a round of EFT for a positive, an antidote to your particular kinds of stress, so the lady who asked with her big nose, "What kind of positive would you need to never have to worry about your big nose ever again?" The lady might say, "Beauty. I just want to be beautiful. I am so ugly and I want to be beautiful, and if I was beautiful then I would find love."

Well let's tap on that. Let's tap on, "I want to be beautiful."

We make that declaration in the Heart Position, and then tap all the points with the reminder phrase of, "Beautiful."

With this lady, somewhere during the round of EFT the wording began to change, to "I am beautiful." And at the end only the word itself remained, "Beautiful ...."

It was then that she opened her eyes and smiled. And guess what? She really was beautiful because beauty is not just plastic surgery noses, beauty is a light that shines from within and touches the heart.

Beauty is a light that shines from within and touches the heart.

Beauty and love are interchangeable, for at the end of the day, all is energy, all is love.

Tapping For Love

If you're ever stuck for a positive on which to tap, simply tap for love.

Allow yourself to really want more love in your life, open yourself to allowing the energy of love itself to transform you, use your own words and try simply "tapping for love."

Here is an example of evolving the concept as we are tapping through the points.

I want more love in my life.

I want more love for myself.

I want more love for my friends, and my loved ones, for my family, for my children.

I want more love for my partner.

I want more love for all the people on Planet Earth.

I want to experience more love.

I want to be able to give more love.

I want to be able to experience more love.

I want to be able to notice love all around me, all the different variations of love.

There is so much more love for me out there.

Love in its widest metaphorical sense, love emits the widest frequencies, expanding way beyond just the colours of the rainbow, all the different shapes and forms of love. I want them all and I open mself to all the love in the universe and beyond, and beyond, and beyond, and beyond!"

This is just an example of how to expand a simple tap on "love" into a real energy experience as you let your ideas start to flow and really "get into" what that positive means to you.

Try this for yourself now.

Really, it only takes a few moments.

Take a deep breath, place both your healing hands of energy on the centre of your chest, and simply start with, "I want more love in my life ..."

Now, how do you feel? Calmer? Clearer? More philosophical?

That's a good start but *love is even more than that*.

We are used to equating love, or real love or proper love, with heart break and young people from warring families, poisoning and killing each other in their desperation. "Love hurts" is what I saw on a T-shirt slogan one day.

It is true that when love goes wrong in the old sense, we do experience the most extraordinary heart break and we humans can even die of a broken heart when it gets bad enough. That too is true, yet the true nature of love is not suffering or writing long heart rending poems in the middle of the night, with the quill dipped into your own heart's blood.

The heart of love is sparkling, it is light, it is explosive, it is like a fountain, it is joyous in the extreme, and for us to touch that joy of love, that lightness, that delight of love is the next step on our journey.

Love & Happiness

Love brings happiness. That is a fact, even if you had a lot of bad experiences with love, or it has never worked out for you before. It may be your experience instead that people have trampled on you, hurt you, disrespected you, or you've been in many relationships and it's never been as you've dreamt it to be after high hopes.

Or perhaps you haven't been in any relationships at all, and you've given up on it altogether, "Love is not for me in this lifetime."

It doesn't matter. At the end of the day, we all want more happiness and if we focus on using energy to bring this about, we are playing a whole new game.

So, and no matter who you are or how good, bad, or non-existing your love experiences have been thus far, let us have a tap on happiness, to put happiness back together with love, to renew and strengthen that essential connection between them because ...

Love <u>is</u> happiness.

Put your hands on your heart, take a deep breath in and out and consider those two positives together, love <u>and</u> happiness. Take your time and mindfully tap all the points, seeking to increase that energy flow you can feel in your own body as you consider happiness and love. Let words come to you as you tap to express yourself, your thoughts and feelings on the topic.

Focus on your desire for experiencing the lightness and the happiness that love brings. Let your desire build up to be more deeply in love, more often, for when you are in love then all things become beautiful.

If you have never been in love you will have to take my word for it, but everybody else, you know what it's like when you are in love. The colours are brighter. Gravity doesn't exist, there's magic in the air, birds will literally land on your outstretched hands, and little children smile at you as you don't just walk by, as you glide by in this state of utter joy and happiness. That's the kind of state of being we are aiming for as we seek to raise our energy levels even higher.

So now, and in this spirit, let's tap for happiness, and please use your own words to qualify, expand and shape the concept as you tap through the points.

Here is an example:

I want more happiness in my life.

I want more happiness for me.

I want more happiness for my friends and family.

I want more happiness in the world, more lightness.

I want to experience happiness in every single cell of my being.

I want to breathe in happiness.

I want my heart to beat happily.

I want to walk and move happily.

I want happiness to be the state in which I work, live and sleep.

So now how do you feel?

Happier, of course - we can sense some smiles around the world now that weren't there before.

Love & Light

We have had an experience of tapping on love, and we have tapped on happiness, so I would now invite you very much, to take that next step and make it even lighter, even brighter.

Love is as light as light itself, even lighter than light.

Love is a light energy.

Love is a light energy. It makes things easy. It makes things happy. It smooths paths. It heals worn out souls if you will.

Love is very light and playful, childlike.

Love is fun.

To connect with the truth of that, let us now tap a round of Positive EFT for light love, for love and fun.

Fearless fun, where all the cares and the worries about learning and educations, and evolution, and spirituality is all gone. it's all behind us and all we're doing now is having these moments of wonderful fun with the universe, with other people, with our loved ones. When we come together and our joy and fun and lightness becomes this true lightness of being.

Especially if your experience of love hasn't been that much fun to this point, take a deep breath, put your hands on your heart and say:

I want more fun in my life.

Let your own desire for the lighter kind of love rise up within you and choose your own words as you tap through the points.

I want more fun and love in my life.

I want more fun in my life!

I want more carefree fun.

Fun and love.

Love that is fun!

Playful, joyful love.

Love filled with light and laughter.

Light love.

Discovering new meanings of fun and love.

New dimensions in love and fun!

Love, fun and laughter.

Delightful love, light filled love.

The fun of love, the joy of love.

Can you feel the lifting and the light(e)ning this produces?

This is one of the most wonderful personal experiences in modern energy work - that love isn't dour or heavy hearted, no matter how intense it becomes. Indeed we can say that until love is lighter than light itself, we've probably haven't experienced the true nature of love or the most mature expression of love ... yet.

But it's out there, and it is awaiting ... ☺

Love & Protection

With that additional lightness that fun brings, that lifting, there occurs a powerful lifting and a movement away from all the suffering of the past. Having not just a powerful energy system, but a light one, quite literally lifts us up and above the normal cares of the day.

It also quite literally gives us a bigger picture and puts our lives in perspective. It leaves swirling fears and insecurities far down and beneath us.

And if this wasn't already enough, there are even further blessings.

When you're coming up to these higher levels of powerful energy flow, where things become lighter and easier, what we also find is that it creates this strong energy field all around you.

Generating this kind of energy repairs your aura, if you want to call it that. It creates a field of protection around you.

This answers the age old question of "Oh my God, what would happen if I became more lovable? Then I would attract stalkers, and leeches and everybody would fall upon me and tear me to pieces!"

This is not the case. The fact is that predators, bullies, leeches and stalkers are attracted to weakness, and to energy systems that are essentially unprotected. Easy prey, in other words.

You might notice for yourself that as we're doing these energy exercises and you're coming up on your energy levels, how much stronger, bigger and more expansive you feel.

You feel physically bigger and stronger, more at one with your body. Your reactions and reflexes are sharper, and you feel as though there is a field of safety around you. This is not an illusion, it is a provable fact and simply a side effect of increasing the power flow through your energy body.

As our energy system starts to power up and especially the heart of energy and the heart of course is what love is all about, the natural protection field becomes stronger and stronger so it answers both the questions, "How do we attract more people to us?" as well as "How do we attract the right people to us?"

I am sure you have heard talk of "raising your vibration" in order to attract more luck, more love, more opportunity and so forth, but it is rarely explained what that really means.

Raising your vibration is nothing more than shifting your average energy state up towards the high positives on the energy chart.

I don't believe we are supposed to be jumping around at +10 incessantly and all the time. We all have our ups and downs, but what we want to try and do over time, is to bring our average up a little bit here.

So if you've lived your life at mostly at -4, with the occasional dip into -6, and just once in a blue moon a little +3 here and there and a true +10 perhaps twice in your life, that would give us an average over your lifetime of -4.

That -4 would be "your vibration" and it's not a good place to be.

We need to bring this average up to at the very least a +3 to get us started.

This is achieved by spending less time in these negative energy states and more time in the higher energy states.

This does not mean that you have to float around like a saint all the time, it just means that if you can stop once in a while, and notice if your energy has gone down too much and you're starting to think things like "This is too hard. I can never make it. There's not enough time. Nobody loves me ..."

All those negative thoughts, they're just your warning lights, your little red lights on your dashboard to say, "Hey you need more energy!"

And right there, you can just take a moment to do something about it.

You don't always have to tap. This is about raising your energy levels, so you can just take a moment, step outside, take a deep breath, look up at the sky - it is always there for you! - take another deep breath and let that energy raise you and lift you. Let it flow through you. Let that momentary lift that you need to bring your energy system back up to some kind of even keel and level functioning.

The more often you do that, the more often you take action when you get these indications, these negative thoughts, the more often you can stop and raise your energy, the higher your energy level average becomes over time.

The more often you practise this movement towards better energy flow, the more you will also increase your range and flexibility, the easier you find it to bring yourself higher up on these energy levels.

Managing your energy body and thereby, your emotional states is what we learn by doing this - and that is the core skill you need for successful dating, for successful relationships and certainly, for successful lives.

Love & Sex

Okay, so now let's talk about sex, shall we?

Before you go to skip this chapter because you don't need it, let me take us back to the reality and the practicality of working with the energy body.

The sexual circuitry is the most powerful energy system we have, full stop.

The sexual circuitry is the most motivational, the most empowering, and the most extraordinary energy sub-system in many ways and when we're talking about *empowering the energy system*, then the power flows that run through the sexual circuitry are just irreplaceable.

The 1st Circuitry, as it is called, is supposed to provide power for life. And when it doesn't work, really bad things happen to our energy levels and our energy averages.

When the 1st Circuitry is out, that is like taking the main power line to your house away and trying to run little wires here and there from the next door neighbours out of their sockets, so that you can get your fridge to work, or your TV to run. Or your cooker, your heater, your washing machine - but you have to make up your mind which one you want to be using because there's never enough power to make it all work as it was designed to work, and there's a constant threat of short circuits and fires.

All societies have their own way of suppressing human sexuality and sexual energy. And there is not a one amongst us who has a fully adult, fully actualised 1st Circuitry. *First* circuitry, the energy flows that are driving creativity, survival, procreation, sexual competition and all of that.

Without the 1st Circuitry working and being able to flow enormous amounts of energy through it on a regular basis, we have a real struggle on our hands to keep our energy system running as powerfully and as high as it should be running. In fact it is my supposition that it is primarily damage in the 1st Circuitry, above all else, that is causing people to feel so powerless and spending their entire lives at -5.

If we were to make a list of our sexual traumas, our sexual problems, our weird and dissatisfying sexual experiences and all the reasons why we have these, we would be lying on the psychiatrists couch until the end of time.

Luckily, we're not psychologists, we are energists here, and our concern is only with empowering our energy body.

We achieve this by increasing our X Factor, bringing us into a position where we can love better, love more easily, love more joyfully, love with more lightness and fun, more certainty and in far more safety.

When you start to "think energy" it is obvious, unavoidable that people who try and find expression for their sexual energy from a very low energy state are going to have bad experiences with sex. There is just no doubt about it.

You know you're not firing on all cylinders at -3 or -4.

You might be picking the wrong partners. You might be needing to use substances such as alcohol or drugs possibly, to get you in the mood or get you over your fears of reversals in the first place. And you know there's all this swirling doubt and fear and that is not a good place from which to make what can be life changing decisions and certainly not a place from where we find entrance into the holy expressions of sexuality, the absolutely numinous, totally mind blowing experiences of sexuality.

So even if you never to desire to ever have anything to do with sex again, I would strongly encourage you for the sake of your mental, emotional, physical and most of all spiritual health, to join us here as we just consider for a moment what we can do to help our 1st Circuitry work better.

This is only about the energy flow in the energy body; this has nothing to do with going out and having sex with anyone at all. This is about simply finding some kind of energy vitamin, energy cure, a positive antidote for whatever has gone wrong in the past.

People often say, "For me to even get started on a journey towards becoming a fully functional adult, an amazing lover and a fully actualised sexual being - well, *that would take a miracle*."

Love & Miracles

And of course - what is the greatest miracle?

Love.

Of course ...

In this spirit, let's have a tap of Positive EFT for miracle - just so you can find out how that feels and what it does for you in the context of your own sexuality.

"My sexuality is a miracle. I want to have miraculous sexual experiences in my life."

We are going to tap a round on miracle, and hold in your mind that you want to explore the miracle of love and sexuality. Expanding the concept of love, love in its widest metaphorical sense which then includes physical love as well. I don't mean by that necessarily having sex, it can be a loving touch, simply a physical expression of love.

So let's just tap on the miracle of love here, and as we do, we understand that this isn't one single miracle in a lifetime, but a progression of miracles, each one better than the next, as our concepts of love evolve and our capacity for love evolves with every miracle that comes our way ...

Put your hands on your heart, take a deep breath and choose your own words, as you tap, focusing on the miracles of love.

I want to experience more of the miracles of love.

I want to explore the miracles of love.

I want to unlock the power of the miracles of love.

I want to bring the miracle of love into my life.

I want to bring the miracle of love into our life.

Love in its widest metaphorical sense.

To experience the miracle of love, in my body.

I want to experience the miracle of love in my body.

I want to be able to give and receive the miracle of love.

Give and receive the miracle of love.

Love is a miracle, a miracle.

Now how does that feel?

Love, Sex & Light

Very good, and now - do you remember the lightness?

Let's bring in the lightness of sexiness, the delicious, tingling delight when the sexual circuitry starts to come into life, and with it, our entire mind/body/spirit system.

Love and sex are not just about the heavy duty soul mate stuff and having to have religious experiences, that's just one aspect of the wonderworlds which await us here.

When we remember the lightness, we really experience the lifting.,

Light and sexy.

Let's free ourselves from the old shackles of making sex terrifying, dour and miserable, rise above that, take wing and in the energy worlds, get to experience the power of light, sexy energies to bring us to life, to put a smile on our faces and make us glad to be alive.

Let's just tap a round and be more sexy so you can have an experience of that.

Put your hands on your heart, take a deep breath and focus on sexy energy this time.

Here is our example.

> *I want to be more sexy, and mean that in a light,*
> *happy sense. in a sort of a light playful, flirtatious sense.*
>
> *I want to be more sexy.*
>
> *I want to feel more sexy.*
>
> *I want to feel more sexy in every cell of my body.*
>
> *Light and sexy.*
>
> *Playful, sexy and sparkling!*
>
> *I love feeling sexy and alive.*
>
> *Light as light and very sexy!*
>
> *Sexy energy flows through me!*
>
> *Sexy energy!*

And that's what I call a sexy energy. it's not a sexual energy, it's not a hard core red light district kind of energy, it's that light playful, sparkly sexy touch, that brightens the day and when you are flirting with somebody or when you are dating somebody. that's a perfect, easy, happy, light approach. it's not heavy, it doesn't frighten people. it's attractive, it's light and sparkly and it's fun to engage in.

Excellent!

The seX Factor

So far, we've got the miracle of love and sex, we have been playing with light, happy sexiness, and so now it's time for the big one, which is the X Factor.

The X Factor is your energy system, in full flow, in full blossom if you will. When your energy body has become this fountain of light that radiates from you but also rushes through you, connects you both with the Earth and the sky, powerful, protected, amazing.

When we tap on our X Factor, we leave it up to the energy system itself to sort out what it is we're tapping on. The energy system is a complex and multi-layered place and consciously, we just don't know anywhere near enough about it to even diagnose what's wrong, or where that may be located, never mind what to do about it.

So take a deep breath right now, put your hands on your heart of energy, take a moment to consider just how different and wonderful life will be for you when you can increase your X Factor overall, when your energy body really starts coming to life and providing you with that power you might have been waiting for to come to you ...

Deep breath - I want to increase my X Factor.

Tap this now and if you want, you can think in terms of your X Factor as your seX Factor too because that is certainly a part of it.

Here is our example.

I want to increase my X Factor.

My X Factor.

Wake up my X Factor

My seX Factor

Empower my X Factor

Light up my X Factor

Light and bright and flowing powerfully!

Fresh new energy flows through me.

I'm alive and I'm loving it!

How does that feel? Nice and tingly, and kind of mysterious?

Yes it is, the mysterious "je ne sais quoi," that wonderful thing that just brings that extra dimension of light, and love and potential.

This is the energy that causes sparks to fly, and these can be sparks of physical creativity or sparks of intellectual or spiritual creativity.

The more people can raise their energy levels up, become sexy, tingling and shiny and have this X Factor at work, the more potential begins to exist for all of us, to have these new experiences with one another and evolve.

And they can be as amazing as just a smile flashing across the room, or a light touch with your finger tips with someone else. Right moment, right time, that sense when a bolt of electricity shoots through you from the tips of your toes right to the tips of your hair and out the top of your head and you cry, "Oh I feel so alive!!!" And that's really then the final round of Positive EFT that I'd like us to do in this set. It's all about being alive.

Being Alive

Being truly alive is expanding, embracing and then owning all of your systems, all of your capabilities. Having access and awareness of all of yourself and being connected with all of that, being so securely held within that loving matrix.

So let's just tap around on being alive together.

Take a deep breath, place your hands on your heart of energy and focus on the fact that you are alive.

Become aware of your body and all the sensations, all the senses.

Breathe deeply and if you can feel the energy of gratitude and wonder welling up inside of you, that's just fantastic.

Use your own words, take your own journey.

Here is our example.

I am alive.

Alive and loving it.

I am alive and I am loving it.

I am loving life.

I love life and the expressions of life.

I love life and the miracles of life and love.

I love life.

Life is delightful.

I was made for life and life was made for me.

I am alive.

Alive.

Wonderful!

Your Love Goals

We have established our basic principles of using positive energy and you have had opportunities to experience in your own body, mind and energy system how we can make ourselves feel more alive, more present, more empowered.

This is really as simple as making a heart felt wish to have new and better experiences, to tap while we're thinking about this, and letting the changing energy flow expand our concepts and understanding of core concepts such as beauty, love, sex and light.

This process becomes even more wonderful and even more powerful when you find your own positives of love. These personal positives are the exact right antidotes that you need for whatever has gone on in your life before, the kind of antidotes that are exactly right for you to help you move on to the next step, to the next level, to the next unfoldment.

We have our global positives chart, and it has lots of different powerful positives on it. This is a good way to get started.

In order to discover which positives are the most transformational for you personally, we need to consider your personal situation and your personal love goals at this time.

Lots of people wander through life with sadness and sigh, "I just want somebody to love me," and it's like they have a target on their backs. Those who are on the lookout for this kind of vulnerability will take pot shots at them. A love goal of "I just want somebody to love me and I don't care who or how badly they treat me or how wrong they are for me, I just want somebody to love me ..." is fairly guaranteed to lead to more misery rather than less.

Yet this is only an indication of chronic low energy flow. it's a desperate cry by people who haven't been loved enough, and frankly that's the case for every single human being on the planet today. Nobody's being loved enough, it's the same everyone. Deep down we all feel we haven't been loved enough and deep down I think we're probably all right about that.

However, when we get higher up on the energy chart, what we find is that we were loved, and there was love in our life, and people have tried to love us as best as they could under the circumstances. And when all else fails, of course the great Creative Order loves us all, the universe that has created us and holds us safe, and provides us with oxygen for breathing and the planet for walking around on, and stars to look up at and worship at night.

When we're in positive energy states, we know it is an expression of absolute infinite and indescribable love that we're even allowed to be here and experience these extraordinary things that we are experiencing here.

Therefore, it stands to reason that we need to re-visit our old love goals and replace them with love goals which have come from a "higher place" - a higher state of being.

Take a moment now to sit back and consider this.

What are your goals in love?

Some might be thinking, "Oh I just need to heal first from all the terrible injuries that have been inflicted on me ..." and I can understand that.

There was a time when I might have thought the same, but what actually heals the past is the present and the future. As a simple example, you might have a lady who was terribly treated by her father and then by many boyfriends, and she's lying on the therapists couch and they're doing their therapy thing.

For many, many years and actually nothing changes until one day she meets this man, and he is a counter example to everything that's happened before. And in just one night, he manages to heal that which has been a pain of a lifetime.

Now you could say that the thirty years or so that the lady spent on the therapists couch changed her vibration enough so she was ready to attract this wonderful person, or this person who had it within their power to give her this new experience that overwrote the old. But I would say we don't need to lie for thirty years on a couch in order to change our vibration. All we have to do is to work on our energy system a little bit, every day without fail, and that is really as easy as going outside and taking a deep breath now and then or tapping a round of EFT on a positive, as the case may be.

So if you are of the persuasion that you need to do an awful lot of healing first before you can have these new love experiences, I would put it to you, you know that just by raising your energy and getting into that where you're starting to attract new offers of love, and new opportunities of love, that the healing actually lies in the experiences you are going to have after you're raised your energy.

That these new experiences are what in the long term will eventually heal you, and they are the only thing that can.

If you are not in a relationship at this time, you could make it a goal to "find the perfect person for me right now."

"I am ready for a relationship and I eagerly await the person who is going to help me evolve to the next level."

Please note that here, we are only asking for a person to help us evolve to the next level, not "the one," the one and only soul mate.

For many people, the ultimate goal of finding their soul mate is a huge leap, and in energy work, we have this idea that "you don't have to solve it, only evolve it."

Perhaps a few more experiences are required before you're ready for the soul mate?

Either way, if you have worries, fears, anxieties about going for your love goal, we can simply use the positive approach and ask:

"What do I need to make me ready for love?"

If you can't answer that question yet, we can work it from all the reasons why you can't find love, and then use the positive antidote.

For example, one person might say, "If only I was much younger, then I could find someone ..."

With this person, we can tap for "youth" in order to activate the energetic fountain of youth inside them and as a side effect, change their mind about many things. It is a fact that very young people fall in love with very old people all the time; indeed, people fall in love with people all the time and youth and age has nothing to do with it because it is an energy thing.

Always remember that love and all the emotions that drive people's actions are ENERGY based.

Love is an energy thing and it can happen between any kind of person, at any time.

Allowing yourself to be open to being surprised, what sort of person it is that your heart will lead you to is another aspect of this.

Many people have these very strong Guiding Star based ideas that the ideal man they're looking for is exactly like their father or exactly like their uncle Andrew, or exactly like Elvis Presley, and that's the only person who could ever make them happy.

There is an old saying; you know people will fail live their dreams as long as they continue to dream the wrong dreams. I think a part of this finding the right person for you is to free yourself from the old expectations, just let that go, put that behind you and say to the universe, "Okay, I am ready to meet the right person, and I am going to lay aside prejudices. Lay all the prejudices aside and let my heart and my soul guide me to the right person that's right for me at this time."

What do you need to "get over" your old prejudices, judgements, expectations and templates? Over your old Guiding Stars?

What do you need to free yourself from the shackles of old that have kept you trapped in a time warp?

What do you need to power you up and over the next threshold, to a place where instead of trying to catch ghosts, you can be presented with all these amazing souls, and some of which absolutely will hold the gifts and keys to move your incarnation further and higher than you ever even dreamed of?

What do you need, right here, right now?

Let those positives come to you and start tapping!

You have taken perhaps the most important step to finding out the meaning of true love in this lifetime.

And what a triumph that would be!

Getting Over "Loving Yourself"

Clearing the path to the future from the ghosts of the past by asking for the new, for the next, and what we need to do to take the next step is in and of itself an excellent love goal.

Don't let any perceived barriers to this forward movement stand in your way. We have been entrained to think that somehow, we need to learn to love ourselves FIRST and BEFORE we can expect anyone else to love us.

Loving being an outward bound movement, and that's the only way it can ever flow, makes "loving yourself" structurally impossible.

We can love past aspects of ourselves, and future aspects of ourselves, sending that outward bound energy across time and space where they need to go, but loving yourself in the here and now is as impossible as it is to jump over your own shadow, or to view yourself through your own eyes.

There's no need to worry about that. We can just let that old idea that you can't find love unless you've done the impossible first and once more consider the energy of the situation.

When we come up on the energy scale, we become more loving.

At +5 and above, we will be looking to love someone, rather than looking for someone to love us.

The whole "loving yourself" issue has ceased to exist altogether.

And if you really need to "love yourself," then simply think of it in terms of "That means tapping a round of Positive EFT for something really nice and tasty, which will bring my energy levels right up and all's well with the world.

When you are high on the energy chart, you become the walking manifestation of love and you have it in you to love others. You have become the metaphorical rich man who gives, instead of being the eternal pauper standing with their love begging bowl on the street corner in the blizzard!

Partnership Love Goals

We want to take this stance with partnerships:

No matter how good it is, it can always get better.

Hold firm to that, remember that and never, ever become complacent.

No matter how intense your relationships are, they can always get more intense. No matter how sexy they are they can always get more sexy. There is more. Believe that. Do not believe that it gets less, that the best it can be is when you first got together in the first flush of romance as it's now, and after that it gets all mundane and boring and tedious. It doesn't have to be that way; it can be the exact opposite.

Two people who have a deep desire to experience more of the miracle of love, in mind body and in spirit, have got a wonderful opportunity of exploration and enrichment there. And I really highly encourage that you should take that.

So for couples, please do not make negative goals. Like re-stating yet again, "I want him to stop being such a complete idiot," or "I don't like what she wants me to do in bed," or things like that.

Go for a positive goal in love, such as "I want us to be closer than we've ever been. I want us to be freer than we've ever been. I want us to be delighted in one another. I want to experience bliss with my partner."

Bliss is a nice word, is it not? Bliss, ecstasy, really set the goal high and accept no substitutes.

Surprise is another wonderful positive, especially for long term relationships.

We might think we know our partners inside and out, but we don't. What we think we know of or about our partners is barely the tip of the iceberg. There is this whole other unexplored universe underneath, behind, above, around and its so many different aspects.

This is a wonderful thing when you're of the right mind. There is never any need at all to be bored. Theoretically, you get a different person every time, which makes it sort of very exciting to head in that direction. So that's a nice goal to find out more about your partner. To get more deeply connected, to get more intimate with your partner,

Releasing the fear of intimacy is often a big step in the right direction, but once again, the simple energy paradigm comes to the rescue. Many people are terrified that they might lose power in a relationship, or dissolve to nothing in the couple bubble, but you see, when you get two really powerful people coming together at the same time, lighting sparks, that's all I can say. In every sense of the word, and this sort of power has nothing to do with dominance and submission.

Powerful submission is extremely powerful, just as powerful dominance is extremely powerful, and whether one partner is always in one role or their partner is in the other or these roles switch over time, and according to the needs of the day. it's neither here nor there.

Love is power.

We were told that power is destructive and that it needs to be curbed and regulated, squashed and taken away from people, but the truth is that power is only dangerous in the hands of an angry man.

Power in the hands of a lover, on the other hand, is a miracle and a blessing, and the greatest kind of magic there could possibly be.

By all means, take a moment now and reflect on your personal goals in love, for yourself, for your relationships of the future, to evolve the relationships you already have.

If you get confused, scared or unclear, simply tap on a positive to bring your energy system up so you can think more clearly.

If all else fails, tap for MIRACLE or ENERGY.

This will help raise your energy system. It will clear your mind and just give you that space where you can truly begin to listen to your heart.

What is it that your heart wants most of all?

When your energy levels are right, there exists a strong connection between the head and the heart so that then you have an idea what your heart wants and you can follow your heart. You will be clear and focused on your goal in love.

Let's say for example, you have discovered that your heart wants more bliss: "I want more bliss in my relationship."

We can tap on that and use "bliss" itself as a straight positive, as a positive energy form, which will be an interesting experience, because so often we only have a vague idea of what the words we use actually mean.

When we tap on a concept such as "bliss," it often becomes much more expansive, but at the same time, much clearer defined. As the connection between the head and the heart becomes stronger, and more information and energy begins to flow, we begin to understand how to do bliss quite practically.

It may also become apparent that there are other barriers to bliss, and we might need the boost from other energy forms to get that threshold shift into bliss.

We can then look to our positives and say, "What do I need more of to make this break through into bliss?"

The answers are as individual as there are individual people. For some, the energy that will lift them up and into bliss could be power. For others, it could be beauty, clarity, passion - allow the right positive to jump out at you.

Now tap that positive, and at the end of the round, look back to your original love goal, which was "bliss."

Now what else do you feel you might need to achieve your goal?

Perhaps a helping hand from the Universe itself, fortune or good luck?

Luck is an interesting thing. The most romantic events happen spontaneously and we call that the magic of the moment.

Magic moments are not something you can plan; however, when you are high up on the energy chart, you can be much more aware of when the magic is brewing, when it is about to come, and opportunities for magic, and strangely enough they present themselves almost all the time.

It is really quite remarkable how magical and filled with opportunity the world becomes when we're in the right energy states, in an in-love energy state. When we are stressed and low of energy, our awareness collapses in on itself, we don't know what we're doing and our heads are going crazy, disconnected from the guidance of the heart, we just don't notice these endless conveyor belt opportunities for romance, for being loving, for being light-hearted that are constantly passing us by left, right and centre and all around.

When you are "working" on your love goals, remember the lightness, the magic of love. There is a truly wonderful effect at work when our energy gets above +5 and it is probably related to becoming more aware of how connected we are to everything around us, including our partners and even potential partners we have never met yet.

Opportunity increases exponentially. Luck and synchronicity increases. We become so aware that we start thinking we really are psychic and predict events, as well as create them with ease and with help from the Universe itself.

So when we are talking about outrageous sounding goals for love and relationships, don't be dismayed. You don't have to do this by yourself. As soon as you start "helping yourself" by making a sincere effort to raise your energy levels and bring up your daily and nightly averages, you are engaging in a process that is self perpetuating and then, actively helped and encouraged as surprising, further, unexpected positive events come your way.

The more you have, the more you get given. It's the most fascinating effect but it is real and very reliable.

So and in conclusion to this section, love goals are a wonderful thing.

Write out your love goal on a sticky pad, stick it on your fridge so that it keeps in front of your eyes and you see it there every day, every time before you make a cup of coffee and get the milk out, and keep yourself focused on that desire.

Now this may evolve over time and when it does, simply take the old one down and hang up the new one but for now this is going to help us focus on what we are trying to achieve and keep us moving in the right direction forward on the journey to discover our hearts desires and to follow our heart, and to really find our soul's path here, and find the right people who can help us forward, and move us forward of our soul's path.

Solving Love Problems With Love

Now, let us discover more about the practical uses of working with positive energy, and how we can convert the problems we have into personal positive solutions to those problems.

With positive energy work, it is literally all about raising your energy levels as often as you can and as high as you can, because that is when the magic happens.

When we are stressed and depressed and we're thinking thoughts like ...

- *"I am too (...) to ever find love ..."*
- *"It has never worked before, so why should it work now?"*
- *"I'm just unlucky in love ..."*
- *"With my history, there's no chance of ever finding someone for me ..."*
- *"I am too scared. I am too nervous. I have too much social anxiety to even go out and talk to anybody and even if I did, nobody would ever want me!"*
- *"It's only going to get worse as the years go by ..."*
- *"There's no hope left for me ..."*

... well, those are the moments when we need the positives the most.

In the olden days what we used to do was to then turn to the past.

Let's say a person was thinking about going to a social event where they might meet some other people. They're thinking about it and they don't really want to go because what's the point ... They're feeling uncomfortable with other people. They have a lot of social anxiety. They get nervous. They get wound up and stressed out on one hand, on the other, they are desperately lonely so they put their hopes up that a dream lover will stride into the room and sweep them off their feet ... Which is never going to happen, so it's going to be disappointment guaranteed ... Yet they have to make the effort anyway ...

You know and have met such people, right.

We could sit down and ask, "What's the problem? The root cause? What happened in the past to cause all of this?"

73

And if we do that, we are going to end up with endless, and I mean endless, endless lists of traumatic events in a person's life, of moments where their carers didn't love them right. Incidents and love accidents where they asked somebody out and the other person laughed in their face. Where they were made to feel bad, taken advantage of, were hurt, rejected, betrayed, ignored, abused, bullied, made fun of at work, in high school, in school, in kindergarten, in the nursery, in the womb, in a past life ... It is literally endless.

Any one of us can make lists that are as long as the human genome of all the things that went wrong. And to remember every single one, then to tap through all of those and release every one of those is just such a distressing chore.

To "release it all" would probably take forever, because it is my experience that with every one of those things you release, the next one pops up, and then the next one pops up, and the next one pops up. Unhappy incidences from the past are like the sorcerer's apprentice. You're trying to get rid of the magic brooms that are dancing around you, and then more you chop at them and the more you're trying to destroy them, the more they become fractionated into smaller and smaller pieces until there are so many, you think,"Good God, I could tap a lifetime and I would never get rid of any of that."

In the meantime, time passes and our person is still not going out to that social function. They are still not finding success on the dating site. They are not evolving the relationship that they're currently in. Time passes and they are getting older ... and ever more reasons why nothing is working are becoming apparent and adding themselves to the ever growing list of things to tap on ...

It is important to know that we need to act quickly now.

Time waits for no man, and unfortunately, society has elevated the idea that there is merit in sitting around and waiting for a miracle, for the lottery win, for the knight in shining armour to turn up ... Waiting for the right moment and trusting that the universe will provide and all of that, but the universe tends to only provide those who are aware of what it is that the universe provides, which is usually opportunities rather than fully fledged end results.

The universe has many doors to many futures, but you cannot see them when you are stressed.

For example, if you're getting an invitation to a cousin's birthday party, that's an opportunity. Are you going to take it? How much are you going to take it? When you get there are you going to be aware of what's around you, and the opportunities that exist with people?

You might not meet the love of your life there, but you might meet a person that you get friendly with, and then you're going out with that person possibly just for a drink or to the cinema or something, and it's there that you meet the love of your life.

Life is a pathway through an amazing grid of potential events that we want to travel, so what we're really looking at here is to enable us to do things that need to be done quickly, precisely and positively and to get out of this negative thinking and most of all to get out of that question of "What's wrong with me?" and that feeling that it's all your fault, that you've never found anybody to love you, or that your relationship isn't as fulfilling as it could be.

Just this overwhelming sense of being alone, being alone by yourself or even worse, being alone inside of your relationship. This feeling of being disconnected and alone once again absolutely relates to the low energy states. The higher your energy states are, the better connected you become to the web of life and the web of people too. At +10 you can sense a connection with every living person who's ever been and will ever come to be in the future. At +10, there is no "alone." You feel wonderfully enfolded in this glorious web of all, safely carried in this glorious web of life.

Once you become aware of the existence of this web, you can go out and navigate it at will. Instead of waiting for someone to come to you, you become that magical person that comes to someone!

With high energy flow, you are the proverbial knight in shining armour, which is a metaphor for a "radiant being of light" and the best way medieval people could think to describe what it might be like when someone is that shiny, that powerful, that desirable.

Knights in shining armour don't sit around and wait, they take action.

As we have already discussed, the very first step is to become aware of the energy poverty thoughts, self doubt, negativity, why oh why ...

I cannot overstress how important that is, is your indication to start doing something about it. so what I wanted to do is to talk specifically now, about how to take your own personal negative thoughts, and turn those into a positive that you can use quickly and swiftly, that you can tap on and that you can use as a safety anchor.

I would also like to start talking about how to raise energy beyond even having to tap, because you can't really stand at your cousin's birthday party, see a beautiful man or a beautiful woman, and start tapping. That is just not going to look good.

So now, let us get very down to earth and apply these high principles of love and light to actual reality and we start with your own personal negatives.

- **What negatives do you always think, feel or say to yourself when it comes to challenging situations or any situations in your personal romantic setting?**

It doesn't matter if this now revolves around chatting up somebody, or whether that revolves around getting your partner to notice you more, or getting your partner to do something for you, or having your partner respond to you better.

What are the thoughts and feelings you always have when you get down about your love life?

Whatever that may be, write that on a piece of paper and let's now find the positive antidote for that. And we're literally talking antidote, like this thought is snake venom coursing through your blood, and we're going to inject you with the antidote. The anti-venom that will take that out completely and save your life.

Here are some examples from other people. Please note that the positives they chose are person and just an example, you find your own positives by asking, "What do I need to get over this?"

What you think/say under stress	To get over it, you need ...
"What's wrong with me?!"	ENERGY
"Nobody loves me!"	CERTAINTY
"This is never going to get better."	EVOLUTION
"I'm going to be alone forever ..."	MIRACLE
"There's something wrong with me."	TRANSFORMATION
"There's no point ..."	STRENGTH
"I'm going crazy!"	CLARITY
"S/he is driving me crazy!"	LOVE

When you are seeking positives that will be the antidote to those low energy states don't necessarily look for simple opposites.

For example, there was a person who went to, "I am so ugly," when they got seriously stressed. It always came back to that. Now you might think that tapping Positive EFT for "beauty" would have been the antidote; when that person consulted the positives chart, they found that "logic" jumped out at them.

They tapped for "logic" and halfway through the round had a huge, huge energy shift; they burst out laughing and couldn't stop laughing for nearly ten minutes.

I like this story for many reasons. You can probably imagine what would have happened if we had tried to discover the "root cause" of that "I am ugly." We can predict that the process would not have been easy, that it would have taken a long time, many, many rounds of Classic EFT and probably required half a box of Kleenex along the way.

This took exactly fifteen minutes - and ten minutes of that, the lady in question was laughing and dancing around the room, shouting things such as, "I feel so free ... I've been freed! Feels like an ancient spell has been broken! I feel so alive! I've never felt so alive ...!"

She was literally glowing and being in the presence of that was a delight and a privilege.

Also, her unique antidote, "logic," had jumped out at her. She had known on some level all along what was needed to get over that old blockage or injury, whatever it may have been and however it had come into being. There was a great deal of additional delight and pride in herself that she had figured it out for herself by choosing that positive.

I have every faith in the fact that people do know what they need and want, and are perfectly capable of finding the right positives that will give them these wonderful threshold shifts. I have this faith built on years, decades of experience, including personal experience - and that's the only way to learn.

When you start working with your own challenges, your own repeating stress thoughts and stress emotions, please do remember that "You don't have to solve it, only evolve it!"

Sometimes, you need a cocktail of positive energies to completely solve a problem in your energy system.

You can start with any positive, because you can never tap the wrong positive.

If you need more, simply keep asking, "And what else do I need to get over this, once and for all?"

Make your own personal sequence of positives, each one lifting you higher, and the breakthrough has to occur eventually.

That's a basic principle of Energy EFT and with a little practice, you can learn to trust in that.

Here is another example, this time how to use positive energy to get something done "in the real world," with instant effects.

Here we have our person who suffers from social anxiety, is very lonely and got an invite to their cousin's wedding.

When this gentleman got the invitation, he noticed immediate stress and his own old stress thought, "They don't really want me there. Nobody cares and nobody wants me."

He checked the positives list and found to his surprise that "faith" attracted his attention.

He tapped on "faith" which led to "faith in myself," and "faith in the Universe."

All of a sudden, the invitation looked a lot more inviting. He started to look forward to it and noticed new thoughts coming in which had not been there before. For example, "I haven't seen my uncle for many years. I wonder what he has been up to and I haven't met his new wife. I'd be excited to meet her. She's got two children as well. I haven't met those children. I would like to meet them, to have more connection with my family."

As he was thinking about it, he noticed he got very nervous again. This time it was, "What if there's someone special there? And what if they're already married? Or hate me on sight? It would be too terrible ..."

This time, it was "lightness" that attracted his attention, and he tapped on that. He reported that it was a sensation as though a burden lifted he never knew he'd been carrying for so long. He breathed a deep sigh of relief and then started to smile.

After all, he had decades of practice in finding attractive people who were already in a relationship, and/or who hated him ...

In the spirit of positive energy work, he consulted the chart one more time, and this time, found that "freedom" caught his eye.

Afterwards, he said, "I had this amazing realisation on freedom, that I had so much freedom, so much choice. There was no rush. The desperation had gone completely. There was this deep, powerful sense of, I will find not just someone, but the right someone, and it will be soon."

He attended the wedding and had a good time there. All the relatives were very pleased to see him and many commented how well and happy he looked. At the wedding, he started talking to a friend of the groom's family which led to a new job, and this in turn led to meeting someone who worked there.

This is a classic example of this matrix of connections, of possibilities, that really exists but which we cannot access, know, understand or use when we are in low energy states.

Using positives to address your own personal energy challenges, or emotional challenges, is extremely interesting, easy, and feels so right.

It's a delightful thing to be doing and it re-trains us to think very differently than we did when we kept looking to the past to provide us with clues as to what will happen in the future.

It is understandable how that happens, but it's up to us now to do it in a different way, in a more logical way, in a more loving way.

When love and logic become perfect, they are one and the same.

Love Everywhere ...

There is a concept which is called "Trusting the day and trusting the night."

What that means is that everything holds innumerable opportunities for you. The wider our focus becomes, the more aware we are of all the people around you, the more opportunity exists for love in all sorts of different shapes and forms.

When we are stressed and unhappy, our focus collapses and becomes smaller and smaller - we develop stress tunnel vision.

When it comes to love, our stress focus might collapse so we can only "see" our current partner, who becomes "all the world."

If we don't have a partner, we might be looking for "the one" - a fantasy, a dream partner created by imagination and Guiding Stars from the past, a construct of what we think will make everything alright and so we'll live happily ever after.

A stressed person will go out into a crowd of people and dismisses people, one after the other. You're not "the one," and you're not it, and you're not it, no, no, God no. Not you, not you, not you... until we're left with "there's no one here."

The truth is that there's a room full of people. There is *everybody* here. There may not be the one lifetime soul mate, but there are people here who can provide you with insights, with experience, with a smile, with a story that you haven't heard before, with the potential of friendship. If you already know these people, with a chance of reconnection, with the potential of one of these people inviting you to go bowling with them and your soul mate is at the bowling alley that day. Here is this web, this tapestry of ever spreading opportunity that surrounds you and it also provides you with the opportunity of giving and receiving all sorts of different kinds of love.

Love is not just about sexual love with that one partner, although it is very understandable that it feels like that. It feels like that to people in a relationship and people who don't have a relationship and are desperately seeking one. It feels like that one soul mate sexual endless romantic love is going to take care of everything because we are low of energy.

The fact is though that it takes a village to raise a child.

It takes a village to heal a person, and it takes a village to give us all the different experiences of love that all together make us wise to what love actually is.

Love is being friendly to an old person. Love is accepting a compliment from somebody and not slapping it back into their faces but actually taking it and beaming back at them, "Thank you so much, you made me feel so much better."

Love is standing with somebody and honestly listening to them, that is something all the stressed people cannot do, and by doing that, giving them the sense that they are actually important and someone cares that they're alive.

Love is being flirtatious with an old lady who is sitting by herself in the corner. Light-hearted and just making her laugh, making her giggle like a teenager.

Love is being brothers, being friendly, being patient, being kind, there's so many different ways of love apart from just "the one" eternal romance.

All these different kinds of love are enormously empowering, but more than that, when you are in a relationship with someone, all these kinds of loves come into play.

Yes, so we have our heavy duty Romeo and Juliet, and the bliss of the fabulous orgasms and all of that, and that's wonderful, but that is not the complete picture. Indeed, the expectation of the hard core endless romance is a huge barrier to having a far wider, far more satisfying relationship in every sense of the word.

Love has many ways and the complete experience of love embraces and celebrates them all without reservation. The moments of brotherhood. The moments of flirting, and touching that original sparkling champaign excitement that was at the beginning of the relationship.

There is the care and patience that the parent would give to a child when the partner is upset or ill, or stressed.

There are all these different kinds of loves of the village that we can then apply to the person that is most special to us. So I would highly recommend to practice loving in all its many different disguises and on as many people as you could practice it on.

"Practising the art of love" starts with the loving heart and then possibly a smile with eye contact and attention, a smile for the checkout assistant, saying thank you to the man in the supermarket who puts the trolleys away, a smile, a loving and a blessing for the homeless guy as you put a dollar in his tin. Holding open a door for someone as though they were a king or a queen, sincerely thanking a merchant for the quality of their wares.

Taking the time to comment on something that might seem routine or not worthy of attention. Giving someone positive feedback. Wishing someone good luck and really meaning it.

There are so many opportunities for practising these short flashing moments of love.

When we give out any form of love, it makes the generator that is our heart of energy kick in and flow forward and outward, in the right direction.

The more we "exercise" our hearts and "practice" that outward movement of loving someone, blessing someone, the easier it gets and the better it feels.

The more powerful it becomes, and the feedback you get becomes likewise, better and better.

When someone smiles back at you because you've touched their hearts, and especially if that person hasn't smiled at anyone in years, you receive a gift in return - a gift of energy that serves to empower you even further.

It's an upward lifting spiral, and someone has to start the ball rolling. It's going to be you, and me, and the other energists who have learned that loving is important, that in order to be loved, we need to get ourselves to a point where we actually have some love to give out.

The more you have, the more you have to give.

And the more you have, the more you get given.

Both are absolute laws of the energy universe on which we can rely.

To sum up this section, the advice is to go out there and practice your loving on as many different kinds of people as you can.

It makes no difference if you've found your "the one," if you're not sure and are in a relationship to wait out time until "the one" arrives, or if you haven't found a person to couple bubble with as yet.

Being in a relationship does not mean you can relax now and stop learning about love!

Indeed, people who do that find themselves on the sad end of the divorce statistics, sooner rather than later.

Every time we give and receive a little love in the village, we learn something we can take back into the relationship. It expands our experience and bandwidth of loving.

If you haven't got a relationship, it is just as important to stop filtering people out in your search for "the one" and starting to practice your loving every day, with every one who comes your way.

That will give you a baseline of competency in love that will come in handy when the moment comes and "the one" walks into your life ... :-)

The Love Evolution

To sum up the most important point of this particular set:

We want to learn to make this forward movement from instead of asking, "What's wrong with me and why?" and getting stuck with that, getting sucked into the past, to think instead, "Okay, this is the problem, but now what kind of energy would allow me to overcome this problem? What do I need to solve this problem? What will evolve this problem?"

Always remember that you don't have to solve it, only evolve it. This is a very important statement. Often time's people feel very stuck in a relationship, in not having a relationship, in the way that they think and feel, in the way that things happen every time and there seems to be nothing you can do to get out of it.

"This is the story of my life ... and I'm stuck in the story of my life ..."

When we've been stuck in the story of our life for a certain length of time, what inevitably happens is that we get very tired of being stuck and we desperately want to change our lives. And we deeply yearn for and dream of massive earthquake-like shifts and changes, like winning the lottery, winning American Idol or finding a super sexy billionaire who whisks you off in her private jet to the shores of tropical islands ...

These massive life change fantasies are simply expressions of the desperation of the low energy states. When that goes on for long enough we get more and more desperate and we think, feel and believe that we need more and more extreme measures to try and fix it.

It's not the case.

The huge matrix web of opportunity, love and support is always there, and it is always available to those whose energy systems have enough power to connect with that.

It is as simple as raising your energy levels as often as you can.

You don't need to put a nuclear bomb into your timeline to free yourself of "the story of my life." You don't need an operation, a revolution, a personality transplant or brain surgery.

You don't need to become a vegan, a monk or commit yourself to decades of meditation, either. All that is necessary to make a little bit of progress so that you don't feel so stuck anymore and that's really one of the most important lessons here we have, and that I really want you to take to heart. is you don't have to solve it, only evolve it.

Every small improvement is a triumph and lessens the desperation and the insanity of the "final solutions."

Every small improvement in how you feel about yourself and the universe at large with all those other people in it gives us something special - it gives us hope.

Hope is one of the most important and fascinating positives and if I could prescribe just one for all the sad, lonely, depressed, stressed, anxious, loveless people in the world today, it would be HOPE.

Hope ignites when there is evolution.

Hope is that light at the end of the tunnel, even if it starts out like a small candle flame in the darkness, far away.

Hope, like love and all the other positives, isn't just a word.

It is an energy thing.

It's real, and it's really, really powerful.

The hope of a better future is an energy movement in the right direction, outward going, forward going.

There is a grand movement that binds the Universe - it moves only forward, never back.

Our energy systems, which are of the Universe, likewise want to move forward always.

We need to evolve.

We don't need to create cataclysms in our desperation to take up the pen and start writing a different "story of my life."

All it needs is a will to go forward, to engage our personal power - a will to love.

Life happens and we all have our challenges. We will all experience low energy states where we say and do things we would never say or do if we had not run out of energy, had not run out of love.

The faster we can get back with that forward movement, the better we will be for it.

Don't berate yourself for coming up short once in a while.

For every evolution, no matter how small it may be, celebrate and give yourself a big pat on the back.

Not only are you making progress, you deserve every credit and respect for even giving this a go.

And believe me when I tell you that using love by any other name to change the future is an exponential journey. At the beginning, it might seem slow, but over time, the changes build up and up, and the rate of change gets faster and stronger and more powerful.

So I am really encouraging you here, especially at the beginning, to simply keep at it.

The prophets were right.

Love really is the only answer.

Unconditional Love

Let us discuss some basic love energy principles, which will give you a guideline through your travels in love.

I had a revelation on the subject one day and it is this.

All love is supposed to be loved unconditionally.

Loving unconditionally means to love someone without putting conditions on it, without expecting them to evolve, without expecting them to heal, without expecting them to love you back even.

That is unconditional love.

We've heard a lot of talk about unconditional love and before we had what we would call modern energy work and the concept of being able to raise our own energy levels to the plus side of the energy chart, unconditional love was a complete mystery to most people and sounded like one of those silly things that the prophets talk about that has no relevance in daily life.

And yet unconditional love has every relevance in everyday life. It has everything to do with how you treat yourself, how you treat other people's aspects, how you treat your aspects of the past, and what kind of experience you're going to have in this lifetime.

We can simply say that **the higher up you are on the positive side of the energy chart the more capable of unconditional love you become.**

The same holds in the converse - the lower you are on the other side of the chart, the less energy you have in your system, the less achievable and the less even understandable the concept of unconditional love becomes.

We can simply say that when you're on the negative side of the energy chart, then you need love, and when you are on the positive side of the energy chart you have love to give. And the higher up that goes into the positives, the more love you have to give. It is very simple and demonstrates our core principle yet again - the more you have, the more you have to give.

That does not just apply to money but very much to energy forms and to this mysterious energy form that we call love.

In modern energy work, love is not an idea or a concept but an existing energy form and an absolute non-physical reality.

It is a very hard hitting non-physical reality. There is nothing "subtle" about energy, about love. Babies who were fed and watered but were given no love or attention or energy from their carers simply withered away and died. And the worst people you will ever find are people who share a single constant in their lives. They may have been living in rich houses or in poor houses, they may have been beaten or not been beaten, they may have been starved or not been starved, but the one constant was a lack of love in their lives.

Positive attention, that's a powerful, powerful energy form that human beings need, not just to thrive but even to survive. You are a generator of this life giving energy, and you can hand out if to other people. When you do, it is giving them a gift.

Unfortunately, in our societies we have been taught not how to give this energy form at all, but instead, we were taught how to withhold it in order to control and to punish people. We live in a punishment based society. You can drive safely for 30 years, and no policeman will come knocking on your door to thank you for your safe driving, congratulate you and give you a cheque from the mayor's office of your town. Just once, drive a little faster than you are supposed to, and what happens next ...?

Things have been organised in such a way that the vast majority of the population is kept in a constant state of being deprived of energy, being deprived of love and being deprived of respect.

Children who ask for attention or people who ask for attention are looked down upon. They are considered to be weak and unworthy. And if we correlate that to the energy chart, we can understand why. The energy paupers are the ones who are being looked down upon because they are less intelligent, less capable, have less potential, they're less creative, they're less able to give love or to be relied upon not to do crazy things. So it is understandable how it came to be that energy paupers are looked down upon, shunned and ignored even further.

The problem is though, and this was never resolved by any society so far, that you cannot make a better person by punishment. By punishing a person who is already "bad" (if we want to use that term for anything on the negative side of the energy scale) we simply make it worse for them, and all of us. If you punish a person like that further, what do you get? You get an even worse person. And this applies across the board to people. This applies to murderers and rapists in a federal prison just as much as it applies to people in your life, in your family and you know essentially yourself as well as those you love, your partner, your children and even your pet dog, it is that systemic. It's very simple, by punishment you're creating a worse person and making an even greater rod for your own back in the long run.

We're talking here in terms of energy exchanges, and this gives us then also the converse, because this is a law of nature.

The more you punish a person, the worse they become until they become completely crazy at the end.

- **If you want a better person, you have to <u>give them energy</u>.**

You have to give them love. You have got to find a way to raise them up, to reverse that negative energy situation that is causing their bad behaviour, or their unwanted behaviour, their stupidity or them being accident prone, making always the wrong decisions, holding strange illogical views, having temperamental tantrums, ticks, fits, always ill, always in the wrong.

Whatever it may be that is winding you up about that person or that they're stubborn, angry, aggressive, not cooperative, all of those things are not character flaws, they all happen because people are consistently too low on energy.

To reverse that situation, we need to put energy into the person's system and the best form of energy is obviously unconditional love. Unconditional love is a start up capital and it really means "unconditional" - it is not conditional on the on the person's behaviour, it does not have to be earned or deserved. It happens for "no good reason" and as such works in the same way as a miracle does.

To get a little more comfortable and familiar with the grand concept of unconditional love, let's do the simple thing and tap a round of Positive EFT on it.

When we tap on a high concept such as this, we target the energy blockages relating to concept. We don't know many of these blocks and disturbances consciously and simply have a feeling of disconnect with the concept. We might feel that unconditional love is only for the saints and mere human mortals have no business talking about it. Or that unconditional love is too far fetched to be of use for every day love problems with your partners, friends or children. And it may be true in a way that unconditional love is a high end love goal and a challenging concept, but we can give it a go.

We can shoot for unconditional love and the more we aim for this advanced level in loving, the more we expand our energy system and the better a job we do of loving well - loving our partners, our aspects and other people.

So take a deep breath now, put your hands on your heart and begin to consider the idea of unconditional love - love that is given simply because you exist, and for no other reason besides.

When it comes to tapping the points, do that really slowly and mindfully. Say the phrase slowly and mindfully, speak it carefully and take your time on each point. Let new ideas come to you, but if all you get is physical sensations of energy moving around your body, that's fine too.

Here's our example.

"I want more un-con-di-ti-on-al lo-ve in my life."

I want to experience unconditional love.

Unconditional love.

I want to give and take unconditional love.

Unconditional love. True love, if you will. True love.

Unconditional love. I want more unconditional love in my life.

I open my heart to unconditional love.

I release all blockages to the flow of unconditional love.

I am willing to learn about unconditional love.

I want the experience of unconditional love in my life. more unconditional love flows through me and from me to other people.

I want to experience more unconditional love.

Unconditional love. Unconditional pure, true love.

To finish, always return to the Heart Position and take a few deep breath in and out.

Very good, excellent!

How was that?

How do you feel now?

What did you feel in your body when you tapped on that?

Could you feel energy shifts and sparkles?

Do you feel a sense of waking up, expansion of the colours possibly getting brighter? The slight shift as though you are waking up into a different kind of world?

Unconditional love is really and truly a wonderful thing and the key to so many problems that people have in relationships.

I lay the unconditional love and the concept that *all love is to be loved unconditionally* at your heart from now on.

It's a wonderfully freeing concept on so many levels because it teaches us our love has never anything to do with anybody else but yourself. We cannot control other people, and they can love only as much as they can, but as long as you can love unconditionally, you have the power to always be in love, and it is your power, your choice and your decision.

Loving Yourself

Now here, we are going to explore the idea of loving yourself. You may have heard much said about this, seen much written and it seemed to be only yet another mystifying obstacle on the way to love.

People tell you that you can't love someone else until you learn to love yourself first.

I always thought that this was difficult, to say the least and then much later, I found out that loving yourself is not just difficult, it is structurally impossible.

You can't love yourself. You can't love yourself any more than you can jump over your own shadow - or look at yourself through your own eyes, ever.

One of the BeautyT[2] exercises from EMO that I love to do is to take a person, put them out in front of the audience and say, "Right, everyone! All of you, have a look at this lady.

"Do you realise that she has never, ever seen herself?"

Everybody is quite astonished by this and the audience usually laughs, whilst my demonstration person is blushing beautifully.

I say, "No, really, I mean that. Think about it. She's never ever seen herself at all.

"Not the way you are seeing her as a breathing living, moving, person, a real person, who is here in the room with you.

"All she's ever seen is these flat distorted images of photographs or videos or perhaps a distorted reflection in a pool of water.

"She does not know what she looks like, what she appears like because she has never seen herself, and she will never see herself.

"It is your reflection, in your eyes that tells her what she is because she cannot see herself and as you look at her, isn't she beautiful?"

And the audience always concurs.

---

2   BeautyT from EMO Energy in Motion by Silvia Hartmann, DragonRising 2002/2015, the energist's alternative to plastic surgery.

The truth is that beauty lies in that aliveness, in that real living human being who's breathing and moving, and they're electric and their heart is beating. That and the sensation that you get when you're standing close to them, that excitement, fear that, "Oh my god, who are you? Where have you been? Where have you come from? Where will you go? You are special. You are unique." All of that you can NEVER understand by staring into the bathroom mirror in the morning. You can't get that by staring at videos that were made of you, and you can't get that by staring at photographs.

Please accept that you do not know what you look like.

As soon as you do, a lot of judgement about your personal appearance, your looks, your so called "self image" just disappears and you're left with this question of, "Oh?"

Then we have the other part of this enigma. Physical beauty is only a part of it, and I am talking here to energists who want to have loving relationships, not to people who are totally energy blind, and can't tell a plastic robot from a real woman. Any energist knows that you need MIND BODY AND SPIRIT you are attracted to, a totality where body and mind are some thing, but spirit, their energy and how they make you feel, is everything.

When mind, body and spirit come into harmony or get aligned then you have something so extraordinary, of course it's going to be attractive. Not only that, it really isn't about what you look like, it's about how you can make another person feel, what they feel like when they are in your presence, how they feel about themselves, because they can't feel about themselves by themselves either, no more than they can see themselves, or love themselves!

I figured out quite a while ago that you can't love yourself, and the reason you can't love yourself is that *love is an outward movement*.

Love is an outward movement.

Love is an outward movement that starts in your energy body, flows up and then comes out of your heart centre, reaches across beyond the physical boundaries and touches another person from there.

If you try and loop that outward reaching energy flow back on yourself all you're going to get is a very uncomfortable feeling in the chest and in the stomach.

Don't try and love yourself. You are always the generator of love, the one who gives it in the here and now. You need to receive love from others to experience what that feels like in your own body.

On the bright side, you can give love to past and future aspects[3] of "yourself." They are not you, they are not here and now, and because of that distance, we can send that outward movement in their direction.

We call an "aspect" any occurrence of you through time who is not here and now (yet, or any longer).

All your past aspects are not you any longer. You are not now a three year old child. You look different from that three year old aspect, you talk different, you think different, you have totally different experiences, thoughts and feelings because your energy system has changed so much in the distances travelled that lay between you at three years old and yourself right here and now.

So it makes sense that when we're talking about this three year old, that we talk in terms of an aspect. This puts that distance between us - you now, the aspect then. It then that you can turn around and you can contact that aspect, and the movement then is correct as you are giving your love to the aspect, and it may be so that the aspect looks back across time and space, and loves you in return. When that happens, an energy circuits completes inside ourselves and we become empowered.

That is how you can love "yourself" - your whole self which is all your aspects combined over your whole lifetime.

Now we have many aspects, indeed, infinite aspects as we go through life, of course our partners and our children and our family and every person you will ever meet, they all have aspects too.

The problem arises is when you try and "define" a person, who of course through their days and their lives goes up and down on the energy chart.

They're going up and down, and sometimes they're nice and sometimes they're nasty; sometimes they're wonderful, and sometimes they're completely unacceptable, and a pain in the ass.

Thinking in terms of these aspects of people, allows you to be more specific about your children, your partner, yourself. About the aspects that show behaviours that you don't like when they're very stressed. And from that comes our saying that all aspects are created equally, because it doesn't actually matter if you are connecting or giving love to your own aspect or any other aspect from any other person.

All aspects are created equally.

---

3 Aspects Model of Infinite Selves from "Events Psychology" by Silvia Hartmann, DragonRising 2009/2015. Also taught in the EFT Master Practitioner trainings.

All aspects are created equally, they all do the best they can with what they've got, and it depends on how much energy they've got, just how good or bad these aspects will behave.

All aspects need more love. All aspects need more understanding of their states, more help when they get freaked out; all aspects need to feel wanted, and accepted, and respected. All aspects need food and water, as well, and shelter; and in considering aspects we can begin to understand not only what makes human beings tick, but also deep structural, global rules which we can use to make our lives and those of our loved ones a much, much better place, with lots more love at the very least experienced on a daily basis.

We can love aspects. This allows us to target our love very specifically and precisely at those aspects who need it the most, because they were hurt and stressed.

Loving any aspect is an outward movement, outward energy, giving out love to these "people in time and space," sending pure energy to these aspects.

This is a very useful thing on many different levels. It resolves the problem of "How can you love yourself more? Oh! It's simple! You can love your aspects more!"

You can certainly target distraught and injured aspects from the past and find the right positive energy to send to them, to finally heal them or to break a spell they have been under.

Especially aspects of yourself which you now hate and reject, are particularly ashamed of and wish they'd never existed at all, can greatly benefit from a positive energy injection.

A breakdown in a loving relationship with our own aspects denotes a real energy system problem and by restoring that relationship to one of unconditional love, we are doing our own energy systems an enormous favour.

This is the basic pattern to use for your own aspects, but also, for anyone else's aspects - remember, all aspects are created equally.

Think of a past aspect of you you feel particularly disconnected from, or one that you know is still in pain after all that therapy and all the other attempts at healing.

Take a moment to tune in on that aspect, but don't "become" the aspect. There is no merit in you turning into a wailing six year old at this time; you are an adult and you simply gaze across time and space at the aspect who existed then.

Get a sense of that aspect, and what they needed but were not given.

Let a positive come to you, or choose one from the chart.

Put your hands on your heart, focus on the aspect and say, "I am sending you (this positive) across time and space."

Then you tap all the points mindfully and send that gift of energy.

It can help to repeat "I send the gift of (this positive) to you," to keep you focused on the aspect in question.

When you are finished with the round, take a moment in the Heart Position to consider what has happened, and what the aspect needs next for your relationship to take that threshold shift and evolve into simple, unconditional love.

It's a wonderful experience to be doing that, and when you have "done" (healed, reconnected with, energized) three of your own aspects, and you've got the hang of how this works, try another person's aspect.

Even though each and every "aspect rescue mission" is unique, you will find that the structure is the same, every time.

And every time, you will personally witness how the gift of unconditional love and energy helps transform an aspect.

This is an amazing course in learning to love and I hope you will explore, discover and experience this for yourself.

Another way in which you can show love for "yourself" which is particularly helpful and practical for every day life is to love your future aspects.

These are the people that you're not just yet and they might need your help right now, right here and now, to help put them in position where they can succeed.

You have the power in the here and now to smooth the path for your future aspects, to help them, to support them, and to have their back.

So if you are for example, currently alone and thinking of dating or awaiting for your soul mate to appear and materialise, we may ask ourselves,

"So, there is an aspect in the future that is going to come face to face with this extraordinary person.

"What can we give that aspect today to make it so that when it comes, they are empowered and they're ready and they're not going to stutter and stumble or do something horrible or throw a glass of wine over themselves or that person in question.

"What can we give that future aspect today so that they are ready when it comes, when the door to love opens for them, when the moment arises, so that they're ready for action, at that moment.

"What can we give them today?"

The answers are unique and personal.

For starters, we could send our future aspect who may well be absolutely terrified and frozen in their tracks some unconditional love. It doesn't matter if they win or lose, we are behind them, unconditionally so.

This is looking through time and space to that future aspect and saying, "Okay, my future friend, my dear future self, I am behind you. I have your back. I am going to do everything I can, now and also for all the run up time to that moment when it's happened, to make sure that you're ready that when you step up there you will be powerful and glowing and you'll be attractive and your heart will be open to that person.

"I will do my best so you can be high on the energy chart, and your intuition will be right on song so you will really know this is the right person.

"You won't be falling for the wrong one, because you're really, really there and present and you can see all the things that you need to see, know all the things that you need to know, and really follow your heart!"

So now, find a future aspect of your own who might need this kind of support; and if you are in a relationship, you can find one where there is an opportunity for major romance.

The question is the same - What can you give your aspect so that when that moment comes, they're ready and they can make the most of it, and create this star experience with their partner that is going to lift their relationship to a whole new level.

Take a moment and tap one single round of Positive EFT for a future aspect to empower them.

It's an amazing experience.

Let's do it right now.

Take a deep breath, think of a future aspect in a challenging love situation, or any situation, put your hands on your heart and say:

"Future aspect, I love you."

Now tap mindfully through the points and let the energy and words come to you so it is perfect for you.

Here's our example.

Dear future aspect, I love you.

I love you and I am one hundred percent behind you. I believe in you.

You are amazing. I trust you.

I have your back. I love you and I know you can do it.

I am so proud of you. I am proud of not for what you do, but for what you are.

I have faith and trust in you.

I love you. I am right behind you.

I am going to cheer you on all the way. you will do the right thing.

You are powerful, awesome and beautiful.

My confidence in you is unconditional.

My love for you is unconditional.

My amazement at you is unconditional.

My delight for you is unconditional.

My desire for you to have the best experiences possible is completely unconditional.

My dear beloved aspect, I love you. I love you with all my heart, and with all my heart I send you all my love!

See and this is how you love yourself.

Once you've learned how to love yourself then you can love other aspects, because all aspects are created equally, an aspect is an aspect, it doesn't matter who that aspect belongs to. All aspects need love, they need somebody to believe in them, they need someone to have their back, they need somebody to be there for them in moments of crises to give them that all important support and loving energy to help stabilise their energy system, and to help them evolve, to become stronger, more powerful and to be able to be more loving themselves.

Love is like a resonance. If someone has never experienced love, how would they know what it sounds like? You need to ring that bell in so many cases, so that that resonance strikes them and gives them an experience to get them started.

So many of our aspects have lived loveless lives or had such problems with love or such terrible experiences, and there was no guidance, there was not helping hand. We can send it now, that outward movement of love and support across time and space.

Our past aspects don't need therapy, they don't need to lie on lie on the couch and talk about how horrible it all was. What they need is that energy, that supports, that strength that they were never given, that they would have needed to grow up big and strong, and we can send them that today.

This basic principle applies to all aspects, thereby also to our friends, our families, our own children and of course, it also applies to our partners.

By talking and thinking in terms of aspects, the way we think and the way we talk becomes closer to reality. Just saying, "I and you" is too encompassing, it's too global and too confusing. Yet when we start thinking in terms of the aspects, then we also don't fall into that trap, where because "Peter did something bad that hurt me, Peter is bad."

The aspect of Peter, the stressed aspect of Peter who did something bad, that hurt an aspect of you, that aspect of Peter may have been bad.

Then it is that aspect that needs us to send them energy the most, to free that aspect, to help evolve that aspect. Punishing it is only going to make things worse, it's not the answer, not at the energy levels.

So here we have quite a wonderful simple method, by simply sending aspects love, to help a whole person evolve and be different. And this brings me to a very important part of Energy EFT.

You don't have just to change yourself, you can also change others.

That is a truly remarkable benefit of modern energy work, and in EFT, it is called "proxy tapping."

Changing Others For A Change

In the world without energy, you cannot change anybody else, you can only change yourself.

In the world with energy, you can change any aspect at any time as long as you can reach out to them and touch them.

Indeed, tapping for anyone who is not "I" right here right now could be considered proxy tapping.

You are practically tapping for someone else, someone who is not you, right here, right now.

When you use the aspects model to send love and light to aspects who are in need of that, you are always engaged in proxy tapping - and you need to be, because the energy movement of loving someone is an outward movement that you can't loop back on yourself.

Now whenever the topic of proxy tapping arises we have the discussion as to whether you are allowed to proxy tap people, whether it's bad magic to do that, whether you need to ask their permission first before you proxy tap on them. But here's how I see this.

- **All aspects need love. All aspects need energy.**

I also feel it is very arrogant to presume that we can knock any person, any aspect off their true soul's path simply by doing a little bit of love mojo and love magic.

A true soul's path cannot be diverted so easily.

You will know that this is so if you've ever known a person who was suffering from unrequited love. They might have cast a million love spells to turn your intended's heart to theirs, but it hasn't worked, and it's not working for all their best efforts.

- **When you are proxy tapping with love in your heart and most importantly, *with unconditional love in your heart*, then you really can't do anything wrong.**

A love prayer for any person is something that should be allowed in my opinion. We can all do with more love, more often and more of the time, but it really does help if this love is unconditional in nature - and that means sending our love or proxy tapping when we are in a high energy state ourselves.

In many ways, raising your own energy levels to +5 and above is a safe guard for all sorts of nonsense and evil doing that happens when people go crazy down at -5 and below.

At +5, the very idea of enslaving another against their will or their soul's path, or doing somebody harm by proxy tapping and sending them positive gifts of unconditional love, simply implodes. It just goes poof!

- **We are all connected to one another and sending each other more unconditional love is a good thing for you, me, and all of humanity.**

It cannot be anything but that.

If you should have a sincere problem with accepting that you have the power to actually change the way people behave, or it is against your religion to at least attempt to change other people by loving them more, you can tap on that.

What positive energy form would you need to reach clarity on these issues? To have an experience that will settle the uncertainty once and for all, so that you would be completely clear on what you should do?

I am a great believer in putting the "proxy tapping debate" back to the individual and ask them to use EFT itself to find out what is right, and what is wrong.

EFT cannot tap the truth away, it can only make it stronger. And if something can be tapped away, then it was only a belief, an energy blockage, and not the truth.

I trust in that and this has been my experience with thousands of people over the last 16 years, time and time again.

Using Proxy Tapping To Change The Situation

When we use Positive EFT to proxy tap anybody to change their behaviours or do anything else, and we want to be targeting a particular aspect that shows a particular behaviour.

So for example, instead of targeting "my snoring husband," we target, "the aspect of my husband who always falls asleep watching the television and snores loudly." (And who winds the wife aspect who's sitting next to him and trying to watch the show, right up!)

In the spirit of positive, love based EFT, instead of tapping, "I hate my snoring husband," or "I hate my husband snoring," or, "I want to kill my husband when he starts snoring on the couch," we're going to ask, "What kind of positive can we send to whom to change this (unfortunate) situation?"

Who shall we start with? Should we change the wife's aspect, so that she finds the snoring more interesting? Should we change the husband's aspect so that he stops snoring?

As all aspects are created equally and they all need love, it doesn't matter. In this case, and because we are talking to the wife here, we will start with the wife's aspects, the one who is on the sofa, getting angrier and angrier as the snoring gets louder and louder ...

What can we send that angry aspect?

What kind of energy could we send her so that instead of getting all wound up and all stressed out about the snoring husband, that she could just tune it out? What would she need?

This is a true story and the lady herself suggested that the aspect clearly needed the gift of laughter!

The set up was made, "We send the aspect the gift of laughter!" Halfway through the round, the lady started giggling and made the comment she could always put a cushion over his face, and at the end of the round stated she felt much better, and as though there were many options available to her now, including getting a wireless head set, turning up the TV, or telling her husband to go to bed.

That was a good result, but this lady was curious about doing something for her husband's snoring aspect as well.

The question was asked, "What does he need to not be snoring like that?"

As we tuned into the husband's aspect and started to wonder what he might be needing to be happier and more energized, it became immediately clear that he was completely exhausted. His work was so hard, so tough and took so much out of him, unbeknownst and unseeing to the wife, that has soon as he got home, had something to eat and began to unwind, he also began to feel safe.

On the sofa, with his wife beside him, he finally felt he could stop fighting and that's why he fell asleep.

At this point, the wife was in tears and we had not even tapped yet. It was the natural thing for her to say spontaneously, "This aspect needs more strength, more power to do his daily battles in his work which is causing him so much stress and exhaustion."

So the lady tapped a round on strength for her husband's exhausted aspect, previously known as the "annoying snoring aspect." After that round she said, "He needs more love. Love is what gives you strength. And I love him with all my heart!"

When the lady tapped that round on the aspect who was exhausted and stressed, she felt a real expansion and a warming in her heart, a great sense of peace and then she said, "I really felt my heart go out to him. I love him so much! I'll use his snoring to know when I need to send him more energy, support him much more.

"I'd never really realised how hard he works and how much stress he is under, all the time, until just now.

"Him snoring once in a while is ... nothing at all!"

But there was a side effect.

A few days later the situation occurred with both the wife and the husband on the couch. The wife did nothing different but this time, he didn't fall asleep right away, he actually went and sat close to her and put his arm around her, and he put his head on her shoulder, and said that he felt very blessed to have her for a wife. He had never done this before in over twenty years of marriage. A wonderful romantic moment ensued, and what followed was both surprising and welcome, most needed for the relationship as well.

That was a change indeed.

So is proxy tapping a good thing?

I would say it certainly is.

Just be sure to isolate the particular aspect you want to be dealing with, and take a moment to think about what that aspect needs. If you come up with answers like, "That horrible aspect just needs a big kick up the arse. Or a beating round the head with a stick!" then please read that as meaning you are still too low down on the energy chart and you need to bring yourself up a little before you start to tap.

And that's the big tip and the big warning in working with proxy tapping on anybody or anything is to make sure that before you start proxy tapping, you are in a good high energy state yourself.

The Harmony Program

The Harmony Program is a basic principle of working with energy systems, and once you understand it and try it out for yourself, the world will become a much more reasonable, rational and most of all, a happier place.

The Harmony Program simply states that in order to make good things happen, you just have to give any system what it needs and wants.

So if you have an unhappy, dried up plant, you give it water and then it starts sucking up the water and it becomes green and it makes new leaves and new shoots, and eventually it will flower, it becomes a happy plant. We achieve this miracle of transformation by giving simply giving the plant what it needs - in this case, it is water.

Give the system what it needs.

This is the basic principle of positive energy work.

It is so simple and so logical, yet at the same time, it is so dramatically different from how we were brought up ourselves and what we have observed in the relationships of our elders and all around us, and it does need a little bit of practice to get this right.

"Giving systems what they need to function correctly" is a 180' reversal on so much that goes on in our societies today.

We have already talked about attention being such an important energy for life and that people who are asking for attention do so not because they want to be annoying, but because they need attention, because they're low on attention energy.

People showing annoying, attention seeking behaviours are doing the same as that plant which is asking for water by shrivelling up, turning brown, hanging its leaves down and starting to look distinctly ugly and unattractive.

- **Plants need water, and people need attention energy.**

Once that attention is given, the attention seeking behaviour stops. And it's really as simple as that. Not only do the attention seeking behaviours stop, a renewal of growth and vitality and a true flowering begins as the potential of that person is becoming revealed.

It is extraordinary what huge problems this basic, straightforward concept causes to people who are simply not used to it.

We are used to ignoring attention seeking behaviour by ourselves, by our aspects of other people, and trying to punish it or extinguish it by not paying any attention. But what happens is that because we're not dealing with a flight of fancy here, but a real systemic demand for energy, things just become worse and worse.

The systems of people need energy, just like the systems of plant need water. They cannot do without. You cannot train a plant to do without water. It takes twenty million years before a plant eventually evolves that can live with very little water like a cactus. Perhaps we can evolve to a point where people can live without human interaction. But it's going to take a few more million years, and right here and now we are talking about systems, who when they're asking for attention, when they're attention seeking, it really means means they are seeking a precious substance that they need for survival, for thrival, for feeling better in themselves.

What is also really important to understand is that attention seeking behaviour escalates.

You start off with just a look, or a little, "Hello there," a little word, or a sign or a wave of the hand.

If this is ignored, and continues to be ignored as the attempts to gain attention (read energy, read love!) are failing, behaviours escalate more and more.

When the energy levels in the "attention seeker" get low enough, the entire mind/body/spirit system goes into meltdown and we get into screaming tantrums, fits, rage of epic proportions, physical attacks, and people being put into prison and hospitalised.

What we want to learn is how a stitch in time saves nine. A little bit of attention at the right time when it is first asked for makes all the difference in the world.

This brings us right back to the principle of "The more you have the more you have to give."

The higher you are on the energy chart, the more aware you are of who is in need of attention and their attention seeking behaviours on the one hand, on the other hand the more capable you are of giving an injection of attention energy when it is needed.

For example, let's say you're sitting there and reading your newspaper in the morning and your partner or your child walks in and says, "Good morning."

It is common practice to be annoyed at the intrusion and therefore, to try and ignore that person, to get rid of them as quickly as possible by just muttering something, and to try and blank them, try and block them out.

And what happens? The partner or the child gets angry. Well, of course they will, because they have just asked for attention, for an important, life saving commodity and you have refused to give them this.

They have asked, "Can I have some attention please?" and you've said, "No. Get lost..."

Of course they're going to get what we are used to labelling as "angry," but it is in fact a low energy state.

They have just become even more stressed because they did not get the energy they really need.

Looking up from the paper, looking directly at them, smiling at them, and saying, "Good morning," is all that is required to stop an attention escalation process.

They got the attention they sought; they will smile back and all will be well with the world. There is now positive energy and good feelings, instead of anger in the room - and in the relationship.

Attention is amazingly powerful. It is how we direct our energy to someone or to something; it creates that pathway through which energy flows. So what we want to do, is we want to pay attention to the attention seeking behaviours of our own aspects and of the people in our environment first of all.

Learn what it looks like, sounds like and feels like when people get stressed, and start thinking about the kind of energy that is needed to help their energy bodies work better.

This works both in the moment, in the field, but we can also create significant forward movement by targeting specific energy forms that a person may be needing.

For example, gangsters the world over always say, "I want some respect. I demand your respect!" And they get really upset and even ultra violent if they feel they have been "disrespected."

If a person always says they want respect, what kind of energy do you think we could proxy tap for them? What kind of energy could we give them? What could we tap on for them? Well obviously, respect!

If somebody always says, "You never listen to me." What kind of positive could we be sending them? "I hear you. You are important. Your opinion is important. I hear you."

In what they're asking for, people give you the very key to what it is that will move them on.

What it is that they need to heal, and this applies to your own aspects?

If your own aspects are always complaining that, "Nobody understands me!" then send them understanding.

The words or the way that we express these energy needs is the key to getting this right. One of the core precepts of EFT specifically is to listen carefully to the words the person is using, and then use those exact words, because those words will work with the person who said them.

So have a little think in a moment of, what in your life, you know you, your own aspects, what it is that they are always asking for? "I don't feel supported." OK! Let's tap and send them powerful, heartfelt support.

Somebody said, "You just don't value me." So what they need is to know that they are of value, that they are precious, and we can tap for "value" as a positive. "I value you. You are precious to me. Irreplaceable. I value you for the treasure you are ..."

Give people what they need and they want, and they will be happier people. Like, "I want some respect. I want more support. I want you to be kinder to me. I want you to value me. I want you to love me ..."

These positives are then what we can send a person, and in order to fill them up with that life energy that they need. And I want you to really think of this, in terms of *providing for somebody*.

When we provide for somebody we love, it's not just putting food on the table, a roof over their heads and clean socks every day - that's not enough.

- **Material comforts are only half of what a person needs in a relationship.**

They need those visible thing, that money, that food, the warm, cosy room, those material comforts to physically survive.

But just surviving, just hanging in there by your fingernails, that's not living a good life.

We were made for joy not for suffering, not for scratching around, not for hanging on by our fingernails.

For life to get really started, which it doesn't until you get to at least a plus three or a plus four, we need energy. That's when we wake up, that's when life even begins. For that to be happening we need to provide not just material goods, not just food, not just money, but so importantly provide that energy nutrition that people's energy bodies need in order to work, and keep working and be powerful and attract others, and have something left over to give to others.

The more you can give to the others in your life, the more amazing they become, the more they have the power to surprise and delight you, and the more they have to give to you in return.

This is an enormously empowering and upward lifting spiral.

When somebody asks for what they need or want, even if they're stressed and they're screaming at this point, just take notice and try and provide that.

At the energy levels, it isn't difficult. It doesn't cost anything and it hardly takes any time.

Energy is absolutely free and hugely abundant.

Energy is the most precious, most delicious, the most healing, the most exciting and yet it is also the most abundant thing we could ever dream of.

We are all potential energy billionaires and spending just a little bit of those billions on empowering others lifts us all and makes such an enormous differences.

Find Something To Love ...

Now, I would like to sum up briefly the main principles we have discovered so far.

The first thing to remember is that this is not psychology.

We are talking about modern energy work which concerns itself with the energy body. We've started out by saying that the affairs of the heart, of dating, of love and relationships such are matters of the energy body; they're not matters of the physical body.

Love is not a matter of the mind.

Love is not a matter of the mind. The amounts of people who have tried to fall in or out of love or control their emotions using their mind and have failed miserably are legion.

Love and all it concerns, produces and touches, in its presence as well as in its absence, is our speciality as modern energists.

We actually hold methods in our hands that humanity seems to have never had before.

We cannot master love, but we can learn to flow with it.

We can remove barriers to love, and we can put ourselves into a better position to better be able to give and receive love.

Energy relationships are absolutely amazing and it starts with ourselves and getting ourselves to the point where we are understanding that we're not doomed as a species to endlessly hurt and main one another forever.

There's nothing wrong with us actually. We're just normal human beings in the overwhelming majority.

It is a fact that if a lot of things have gone wrong for us, and most of this is simply due to the fact that we were systemically and chronically deprived of energy. We spent too much time in low energy states, literally crawling about at the bottom of the tank of human happiness.

The most important thing for you to understand about yourself, your aspects and other people and their aspects, is that at the low end of the energy chart we will find the worst behaviours that humans have to offer.

The dark "side" to humanity lies on the wrong side of the energy chart. +10 is heaven and -10 is hell.

Energy deprived systems become ever more extreme as they try harder and harder to gain the energy they need to survive; and this is a simple fact of life, a fact of nature itself, across the board.

It applies to all social mammals, it applies to pot plants, it applies to a single human being and it applies to whole societies as well.

The remedy for that is to put more energy into the system. There is no other remedy. Just as a plant can't survive without water, people cannot survive and thrive and blossom without love.

If you understand that simple principle and apply it to yourself, then you will have a good reason to stop berating yourself or stop taking it seriously when you start thinking thoughts such as, "I will never find true love."

You could ever only be thinking that because you are low on energy.

Take some steps to improve the flow of your energy.

We can start with our list of positive energy forms and simply tap on those. This will lift you, allow you to take a deep sigh of relief, begin to uncoil a little, come to life again.

There is an even more powerful method and this is the one I would like to close this section with.

Love is an outward movement of energy from your heart, and when your heart spins in the right direction, like this great waterwheel, the entire energy system comes back to life.

Take a deep breath and find something to love.

What do you love?

What gives you strength, and joy, and power when you tune in that direction?

What do you love?

Some people love nature. Some people love their partner, or their children.

Some people love sex. Some people love the stars. Some people love the ocean.

Some people love their pet dog, or their cat.

And there are other things to love. Some people love Star Trek, or Elvis Presley. Children might love their teddy bear, and a holistic healer might love their spirit guide. There are role models, saints, prophets, gods and angels - a world of beings, existences, people, energy forms to choose from.

Everybody, no matter who they are, have something or someone they love.

Try it out for yourself, right now.

Find something to love, and let that come to you right now.

Take a deep breath, put your hands on your heart of energy, close your eyes and think about that which you love.

Name it softly and gently, and start your round of Positive EFT, slowly and mindfully at first, then with gathering energy, joy and conviction as your energy flow increases.

It's a wonderful thing in its pure power and elegance of simplicity.

When you have had your own personal experience of the truth of this, you can't help but look at the whole world, and your own experiences up to date, in a very different way.

You find a different interpretation and understanding about why things were the way they were, and you will find a logic to how people have behaved, and why.

Most of all, as you begin to experience for yourself that expansion in mind, body and spirit the higher energy states bring to you, you begin to appreciate how easy and elegant real change can be.

- **When we begin to engage "the power of love" in our practical, daily lives, miracles can and will happen.**

Old limitations dissolve. Negative self beliefs disappear like the shadows of the night when the sun rises. Self destructive behaviours simply drop away, not being needed any longer. Old injuries are healed everything can change, and change EFFORTLESSLY simply because the energy flow in your energy body, has improved a little.

You don't have to wrestle your demons any longer, nor endlessly fight with yourself and the world around you in a bitter battle to the end.

If you can understand that principle, that positive energy forms improve the way you think and feel about the world, and you can start to apply that to yourself, you will also be able to eventually apply this to others and when you do, the miracle of love begins to unfold for you.

Finding love, keeping it, exploring it, evolving it and taking it to the next level is going to become a most joyful and exciting journey of your life.

The A - Z Of Love

1st Aid For Love Pain

The emotions involved in proper love pain are a revelation - these are physical sensations of such power, they bring us to our knees, take our breath away, drive tears horizontally from our eyes with such pressure behind them, can make us throw up instantaneously and create stabbing pains and burning sensations every bit as painful as being stabbed or burned in physicality.

It is only those who have never experienced true love pain who can hold the idea that "emotions are all in the mind," or that you can control emotions.

What I am calling "love pain" here are enormous waves of energy sweeping through the energy system and creating these 6th sense sensations which are on the other side of the scale from the little fleeting shivers we call "intuition."

The energy body communicates with us through the medium of emotion; that is the 6th sense, sensations in the body which have no physical origin.

It is extremely important to understand that we need to heed these red alert communications as quickly as possible, and do something about them as quickly as possible, to avoid serious long term damage and physical illness.

When love pain strikes, fast and hard, it takes our energy system down, and with it, our ability to think rationally. We plummet on the energy scale and it is then we need some practised approaches, something simple and easy we can remember in a moment of crisis.

On the bright side, even though 6th sense sensations or "psychosomatic pains" are incredibly intense, they are **ONLY ENERGY** movements and they respond to energy approaches, fast and reliably.

When we respond in the right way to these messages from our energy bodies, the intense pain can leave just as fast as it arrived.

So here are my tips for acute, intense love pain.

1. Remember the Heart Position and immediately when overwhelming emotions strike, put both hands on your heart of energy and "hold your heart." Breathe. That's the most powerful and instantly stabilising self help we know, and it works.

2. Find something to love. It helps if you have done this before and there is a ready made path for your energy to travel. Speak the name of that which you love out aloud and keep breathing in the Heart Position. When you are able, you can start to tap, but keep one hand on your heart until you feel it is safe to let go.

3. The most intense love pain is caused by a person, and the easiest method to get energy flowing again is to tap on that person's name. On this occasion, don't add anything to it - just tap their name until you feel better, clearer.

4. Now you can use positive energy forms you need to bring you back on track. Simply think in terms of "What does my energy body need to be strong and happy, right now?" accept the answer, and tap that positive.

At some time later, when you are settled and feeling reasonably in the flow, consider the relationship and the aspects involved.

The aim is to get to a point where you know that this exact thing can never happen again. That's an important step; even though consciously we know that a huge energy event is something that is impossible to repeat, we can get stuck and afraid. It's only natural.

There is one more bright side to this.

● **These huge energy movements that cause such intense love pain are <u>transformational</u> in nature.**

These are enlightenment experiences trying to happen; your energy body is trying to evolve.

By working with the energy, rather than against it, we often find that we have made significant progress on our path and in our own personal journey.

3 Paths To More Love

For every conceivable relationship problem or relationship challenge, we have three (or more!) paths to more love.

Let's just talk about a couple by themselves.

We can help Partner 1 evolve and change, become happier.

We can help Partner 2 evolve and change, become happier.

But there is also that "couple bubble" - an entity in its own right, more than just the sum of the parts.

We can tap EFT on the relationship itself and evolve that, make it a happier entity, if you will.

Every one of these three paths will bring about a forward movement, sometimes even a leap forward over an old threshold where things were stuck.

Do them all three, and the potential for exciting new experiences and unfoldments becomes exponential.

The core question is always to ask,

"What would make X happier?"

- Partner 1 might need respect, power and confidence.
- Partner 2 might need tenderness, happiness and laughter.
- The relationship itself might need creativity, union and play.

This is so easy and so natural to do, and it's so much fun!

The best thing is that you cannot tap the wrong positive, ever.

You might not on the first try find that one positive that gives you a huge threshold shift, a massive healing experience and a lightning strike of more love and excitement, but that's perfectly OK.

It doesn't take long to tap a round of EFT, and tomorrow is always another day.

This basic principle can be extended for as many people as you need. For example, if there are children involved, you can do this.

- What does Partner 1 need to be more happy?
- What does Partner 2 need?
- What does Child 1 need?
- Child 2?
- Child 3?
- And the Mother in Law?
- And what does the whole family bubble need to be a much happier family bubble?

It's simple, safe, and a wonderful thing to do at any time and in any combination.

Changing just one energy dynamic in a family, partnership or group bubble of people has an impact on the entire group bubble.

Changing more than one, empowering more than one person has more. Do them all, and it becomes very transformational indeed.

It only takes one person who does Positive EFT wholeheartedly to get this process started. This one person can tap for their own aspects, and for other family member's aspects, and certainly give their gifts to the entire family bubble.

If anyone else joins in and taps too, that's great; and if the whole family bubble can tap together on some desired positives, taking turns to say what they want more of for the family, that's quite wonderful.

Once again, remember that tapping purely on positives makes having beneficial energy experiences easy, safe, avoids psychoanalysis of self and/or others, and brings more love into your life.

It also reduces stress, and completely avoids many of the old problems that seemed so stuck and unresolvable.

Annoying Behaviour

Annoying behaviours in long term partners were always easily treated with Classic EFT - "Even though he/she drives me crazy with X, I deeply and profoundly love and accept him/her." A few rounds of that, and a noticeable relief came into being.

When we use Positive EFT, we are really going for unconditional love and a big threshold shift of some kind. Threshold shifts are high energy events that are unpredictable and delightfully surprising in their outcomes.

Before they happen, and from the place we were, we cannot foresee them at all - they are quite literally "outside the box." They represent as a form of quantum logic resolution, and that's why we cannot find them by thinking in circles, and focusing on the negative.

Annoying behaviours are very rarely there in order to annoy the other partner; the sensation of being stressed by these behaviours is inside the other partner.

So if you're annoyed, that's your annoyance, even though it feels as though your partner is doing it to you.

We thereby ask, "What do I need so this doesn't annoy me any longer? What energy would make me feel better?"

Have a look at the positives list and choose a first positive. That's easy.

You can also ask, "What kind of person could live with that and not be annoyed by it?"

The answer might be, "Well that would have to be a saint!"

You can use that answer as the positive and tap for "Saint." One person who used this approach spontaneously said, "To put up with that, you'd have to be head over heels in love. Then you'd find it cute!"

They tapped on "Head over heels in love." After the first few points, it shortened to, "In love," and finally just, "Love."

The person said, "When I got to the middle finger, there was this huge warm wave that went through me, lifted me up - it was a wonderful sensation and I knew it didn't bother me any longer."

119

But what happened next was quite remarkable. Without any proxy tapping or saying anything at all, the behaviour from the partner just stopped - as if by magic.

I cannot promise that will happen when you tap positives for a partner's annoying behaviours, but that's the sort of thing we cannot predict, is so delightfully surprising and wonderful about modern energy work.

What I find fascinating is **the potential of relationships over time** when we can do something about annoying behaviours and use them for some kind of evolution, rather than to have to keep gritting our teeth for decades.

Especially in the long term, how much difference is that going to make?

What new levels of togetherness, love and communication can we unlock in this way? And even though we cannot answer this at present, and only time will tell, I would predict that this will lead to relationships which are very different indeed from those our elders modelled for us when we were young.

Arguments & Fights

The first rule for arguments and fights in any type of ongoing relationship, and it really doesn't matter if this is between partners, someone and their elders, or someone and their child, is that only stressed people fight.

Only stressed people fight.

If a conversation turns into an argument, and an argument turns into a fight, we have a downward stress spiral of falling energy levels.

It may appear that starting to freak out and throw the dishes around is a high energy state, but it's not. It's a last ditch effort, it's like throwing an epileptic fit when the system is literally crashing and burning.

Therefore, the simplest way of avoiding arguments and fights is to do something about falling energy levels **before** we're starting to scream, storm out, or go into the silent autistic mode of withdrawal.

Know Yourself, Know Your Partner

You already know exactly what your own signs of energy body stress are and how you show these signs of stress. You also know what your partner's signs of energy body stress are, and how they show those signs of stress.

It might be an idea to really become consciously aware of this, and to fine tune your energy awareness.

- What do you/your partner do on a very good day?
- What do you/your partner do on a good day?
- What do you/your partner do on a so/so day?
- What do you/your partner do on a bad day?
- What do you/your partner do on a very bad day?

This gives you an overview on how energy levels not just "influence" but actually *dictate* what sort of person you are dealing with at any given time.

Good Susie, bad Susie; good Peter, bad Peter.

You have a huge amount of leverage over whether you're going to be dealing with good Susie or bad Susie (and many Susies in between!).

The sooner you intervene in any stress progression, the easier it is and the less effort and energy it takes to keep a person on an even keel, or make them happy.

This is a very important point, please take special note of this.

Every person has their own escalation and it is very predictable if you know that person, when you live with them.

First signs can be such things as tiredness, lack of concentration, mild attention seeking behaviours, attempts at starting a conversation or seeking light physical touch.

Become aware of those and respond FAST.

Give the person some energy by doing something positive for them, something loving. Often, a glance and a smile can suffice to noticeably settle the other person down, produce a sigh of relief and a smile in return.

If you are the only energy aware person in your household, it is up to you to become aware of everyone's stress progression and also, to become aware of what works to head trouble off at the pass.

An important note: Energy body stress doesn't exist in a vacuum. When the body gets stressed, through sickness, tiredness, lack of food, lack of water, the energy system is affected. I had a personal experience of going on a road trip with my new partner and having fights three mornings in a row, when we normally don't fight at all. Took me to the third fight to realise that we were both reacting to skipping breakfast. Once this had been found, we made sure to have breakfast at a reasonable time and there were no more fights in the morning. There have not been any "morning fights" since then and it has been 14 months so far.

Please note that when it comes to stress fighting, there is no right or wrong. Stressed people do not think straight and say and do all sorts of things they would never say or do if they weren't so stressed.

When you are stressed, what you are saying or doing seems reasonable or the only right thing, but that's like someone who's on LSD and convinced they can fly. It means nothing beyond the fact that you are seriously tripping, there's no other reality to it.

The stress itself is the problem. Get a little more energy running through the system, and most if not all arguments simply resolve themselves altogether.

Emergency Stop Positives

A very good thing to have to combat relationships stress is to have a particular positive that applies to your partner, and to tap this many more times than just once.

What energy gift could you give to your partner (or your mother, or your child etc.) which would help them feel happier?

If you are in a personal, long lasting relationship with someone you do know what they need, what they crave most.

For some, it might be respect. For some, it might be power. For some, it might be love.

Take that positive, assume the Heart Position and make the set up of, "I give to X the gift of (...)."

Then tap your chosen positive slowly and mindfully through all the points.

Do this for a few days until your chosen positive is clear and strong, feels present as a real energy **form** when you think about it, call upon it or "evoke it," as the term goes.

If you live in a family situation with many different people, find such a positive for each one of them and practice them until you feel you have the hang of this.

Then you can use that positive to stop yourself from getting angry, annoyed, upset, "baited," or having your switches triggered by that person.

Stabilise your own energy system first, then you can get out of the stress progression where both parties stress each other out more and more and end up in a fight.

The Same Fight, Every Time ...

If you are fighting or arguing, and it's the same story over and over again, we are dealing with some kind of major energy blockage in the couple bubble (or family system).

You might have become used to thinking that you know what's right, and the other person is just in the wrong, but you're a part of a joined energy system that is blocking up in the same place, every time.

There is no right and wrong in the energy worlds, only energy, and the absence of energy. Energy must flow and when it does, everything works better, makes more sense, brings more joy and pleasure.

If you think about the topic/s of the repeating (looping!) arguments, and think in terms of the relationship entity as one single system, what positive does this system need to literally "get over it"?

If you can't think of an answer right away, check the positives chart, pick something and just get started.

Make the set up in the Heart Position, "We want to get over this money fight problem. We need more (abundance, lightness, effortlessness, faith, etc.)." Then tap the positive of your choice on every point.

Now, this is important. You need to tap positives until you really feel in your own body, mind and spirit that something has shifted, that you feel differently.

It's only real when you can feel it's real.

It's only real when you can feel it's real.

That's the big guidance factor in modern energy work; that's what tells us when it's working, when you can feel it's working.

Once this has happened, wait for the next time that same argument occurs, or you get stressed and it happens afresh.

Pay attention! Really pay attention to what is happening, and this time, already start thinking, "We need more (patience, kindness, tenderness, energy, respect, etc.) so this won't happen again!"

Although Energy EFT absolute produces the "one minute wonder" type cures where you tap one round and everything changes, it is thinking in terms of what energy is needed that makes the biggest difference over time.

- **We don't just want to fix problems, we want to evolve as people.**

We want to learn how to love more and better, and how to be much, much, MUCH happier than our ancestors ever were.

If you have the right mind set, every argument and every fight offers an opportunity for evolution. It's simply showing us where we're stuck and can improve our situations by getting more energy flowing, more energy moving. Energy and love are interchangeable.

In this way, we can really go beyond just learning from our experiences; we also get to stay human.

Nobody is perfect, and life is such that of course, we will have challenges and we will get stressed once in a while. Indeed, a world where people are floating around grinning constantly from ear to ear, dusk till dawn and dawn till dusk, makes me feel quite ill!

But once you start thinking energy, and start working with positive energy, arguments and fights are not so scary any longer. We can get over them, but most of all, can use them to evolve.

That's the most precious thing of all.

Breaking Up

I personally see people's relationships in this incarnation as each one being their own huge golden wheel in an infinite space of midnight blue. Some spin faster than others, and every so often some get into orbit with one another and turn at the same rate for a time.

This can be moments, days, years, decades.

And there can certainly come a time when two of these huge golden wheels have gone out of synchrony with each other and need to move on on their own paths.

Having spoken to many, many people from all walks of life, all ages, all sexual orientations and religions, with different backgrounds, beliefs, values and attitudes, I have come to the conclusion now that when it's over, you know it.

As long as you are unsure, it's not over yet.

In relationships, there absolutely comes a moment of perfect clarity, and the more energy aware a person is, the more they know exactly when that has happened.

But even people who will strenuously deny the existence of such a thing as energy, chi or prana have their "moment of perfect clarity."

Something shifts in the energy system, and those two golden wheels are no longer compatible.

When this has happened, the relationship is not retrievable; it is over.

There is nothing that can be done about it; and even if a new and different relationship then develops, the old relationship is irretrievably lost.

The couple bubble which existed is no longer, and both parties have to re-arrange their energy systems to account for that.

It's a bigger deal energetically than you can ever tell from just looking at the physical surface; but there is much we can do for both former partners by bringing in the absolute healing power, restorative power, re-energizing power of (positive) energy.

The three key questions are:

1. What do you need to transition to the next level elegantly and with ease?

2. What does the partner need?

3. What does this relationship need to resolve beautifully and in love and light?

These are the kinds of questions and energy moments I would personally never take on in the lunch break in a busy office. Energy work is a ... yes, I'll use that word, a holy endeavour, and something like this deserves time and space.

I would light a candle, put on some suitable music, and sit down with those questions, mindfully tapping and finding the answers from within.

I would let this ceremony unfold in its own way and let my heart and my mind of energy take me through the right steps until all resolves to love.

Love Is The Only Way

It may seem that breaking up is an unloving thing to do, especially if one of the partners doesn't want to, or feels that this is the end of the world.

True, it is the end of one world, one in-life-incarnation, as the phrase goes; but it is also the beginning of another.

Without the old moving away and into the past, the new has no room to arrive; and it is in the new where the treasures lie.

- **The treasures of the past have already been harvested and experienced; the new treasures are what is still to come.**

We may leave a partner, or we may be left; either way, that person will be a part of your personal history forever, and that being so, loving them with all your heart and unconditionally sets you free and empowers you in a way that "cutting cords" or trying to forget they ever existed, never could.

One way or the other, it is your love; you are the one who is doing the loving, you are the one who is uplifted and transformed by that.

Blessed by that experience.

All the positives are "aspects of love" of course but it is simply so that if you get afraid, if you feel you are losing courage, if you feel alone, forsaken or betrayed, tapping on "Love" will get you back on track - and on your own life's path, in every way.

I reclaim my power to love.

Love is in my heart.

Love is my soul.

Love is in my body.

Love is my mind.

Love is all around me.

All is love.

I am love.

I am love.

Love.

Broken Heart

The heart of energy is the nuclear reactor that drives the entire energy system, and when this central power system is compromised, you will find cascading failures across the entire system.

This includes not just psychosomatic pain that can be extremely intense, overwhelming waves of negative emotions, but also a breakdown in the energy body's immune systems and protective systems, leaving a person extremely vulnerable, powerless and undefended.

Add to this all the problems that come with low energy flow, from disturbed thinking to disturbed physical abilities, and you have a recipe for disaster.

On the bright side, when we apply energy approaches directly to the heart of energy, "broken hearts can heal" and the energy system can stabilise much faster than we might expect or have led to believe was even possible.

In Energy EFT, we start and finish with the Heart Position because that is such a powerful lift for the entire energy system and will generate more power, regardless of the problem.

If you are suffering from a broken heart, finding soothing, healing positive energy forms to "feed the heart" are of the essence.

"Find Something To Love"

It could not be any simpler - the remedy for a broken heart is of course, love. That's the energy needed to fire up the heart and the correct vibration.

Now, we always think that we need to find someone who will love us and make it all alright, but the way the energy system works is that by *us loving someone or something else* this generator of love kicks into action and creates a waterwheel type forward momentum that becomes ever more powerful, the more energy love flows through it.

Especially in moments when you feel too weak or distraught to even start to tap, you can assume the heart position, breathe deeply and "find something to love."

This can be anything you love - an animal, the sky, a crystal, raindrops on the window, but also any person, alive or dead, past or present. The main thing is to focus your mind on love, to think towards love. This encourages that great waterwheel to start spinning in the right direction and will first of all, bring relief, and secondly, give you the space to think of more things that you love.

- **Those things you love the most are your personal highest positives.**

Then you can tap on these personal positives and regain energy flow in your system, sanity, and feelings of being alive, of well being.

This may well not be a "one time wonder" intervention, and in cases of severe heart ache and heart break, or if the suffering has been going on for a very long time, you might want to do this very regularly, at least three times a day, every day.

It doesn't take very long, is highly effective and a good start to healing a broken heart.

As time goes on, you might then find that people become drawn to you who can help you with their energy as well until you are completely recovered, much wiser - and ready to love afresh, anew, and as though it was for the very first time.

Crush

I personally find the term "crush" an insult to the actual experience of the person who has fallen madly in love with someone.

To society and bystanders, it's a crush.

To the person who is having these previously totally unknown emotions and sensations rock their world, it is everlasting love and a time of transformation.

Let's consider what happened here from the energy system standpoint. We may have the proverbial teenage girl on the threshold of becoming a woman, or we may have any human being, anywhere, who encounters someone and - alakazam!

The whole world's on fire ...

Everything has changed in a heartbeat. Everything is new and frightening, exciting, needed, wanted - it's a **cataclysm** and I believe that this should at the very least be acknowledged.

To tell a person who has fallen in love, probably for the first time ever, that these super-intense experiences are "just a crush, just a passing phase, nothing really ..." is, as I said, a total insult.

When an energy system explodes like that, it needs to be stabilised, protected, supported and most of all, loved, not negated or denigrated.

Indeed, many long term "love wounds" originate with first love experiences and can leave a person energetically disabled for an entire life time if nothing is done about it.

The first thing we have to do is to understand that something very real happened here, and that it happened INSIDE of the person to whom this has happened.

It may have been triggered by that person outside, be they a movie star or the boy next door, but the event took place INSIDE that person who is now in a state of high energy and sparks flying everywhere - and that means this person owns it absolutely.

When we are armed with EFT, and most of all, with Positive EFT, a crush is not a problem. We can tap on it. Not to tap it away, either, but to complete that transformation that has made the energy system ready for love.

Read that sentence again - **a first love is that transformation that makes the energy system ready for love.**

It's not meant to be horrible, heartbreaking and painful at all. It just becomes that way because our energy systems are so totally mishandled, totally unknown, ignored and mistreated in our societies as they stand.

Using Positive EFT, we can aid in that transformation, that evolution, that enlightenment experience which is falling in love.

We can say to the aspect, and this may be your son or daughter now, the friend at work or an aspect of your own across time and space, "This is a wonderful thing which has happened! Now focus on that person you fell in love with and ask yourself, what is so wonderful about them?"

The answers will give you the positive energy forms to tap on.

- *"He/she is so beautiful!"*
- *"He/she is so amazing!"*
- *"He/she is so perfect!"*
- *"I can feel him/her in my heart!"*

The kinds of energy movements and energy experiences you get from tapping those **heart felt** statements are truly epic.

And they result in taking away that pain and need, and replacing it with a different kind of love and admiration.

You are heading for unconditional love.

Love without the need and pain is unconditional love.

It's the greatest privilege to experience in yourself, INSIDE, as it were.

It frees both lover and lovee in the most remarkable way.

It's the most powerful enlightenment experience available to human beings, and it is available to everyone who has ever fallen in love.

This may sound amazing, the stuff of saints and prophets, but it's actually nothing more than a reality and a potential in our energy systems.

Take away the need and pain, and all you are left with, is love.

Exes

Exes are a particularly "fruitful" area of exploration for the past orientated, trauma digging psychotherapy approaches. We all have them, one way or the other, and whether it was little Suzie who broke your 4 year old aspect's heart in kindergarten by putting a frog down his shirt, or a love affair that consumed you completely but never resulted in anything at all, of course the exes are there.

Someone said to me, "You can't ever get rid of your ex. Unless you develop total amnesia, they'll be with you forever."

I remember that at the time I was shocked and dismayed; but now, being far older and wiser, I have come to seeing the upsides of this.

All our experiences, good, bad and horrendous alike, all together make up our life.

They will be with us, no matter what.

Our exes will be with us, in our energy matrix and yes, there are connections which were made and which remain.

I have never been happy about "cutting the ties that bind us" and have always sought for a better way.

The better way is simple, and it is the way of love, not of surgery.

We need to ask the three questions.

1. What do you need to get over your ex absolutely?
2. What does your ex need to get over you?
3. What does the couple bubble (the relationship itself) need to evolve to the next level?

With these questions answered, we can tap on the positives we need to empower both to the point where the relationship naturally evolves, where it doesn't hurt any longer, and a true state of forgiveness has been reached.

Forgiveness is when it doesn't hurt any more and all that's left is love.

A Progression Of Exes

A wonderfully simple way of evolving out of orbit with old exes and truly moving on is to make a list of your most influential exes.

For each one, ask the three questions - what do I need to get over this? What does the other need to get over you? What does this relationship need to evolve to the next level?

Don't tap yet - just write the positives down that are the energy charges which will evolve these relationships and empower you.

You often find a theme - the same positive turns up repeatedly, and you will learn something about yourself and those others in a new context.

When you are ready, take one at a time and tap positives until you feel joyful, released and truly powerful.

This is a wonderful pattern that you can apply to other people who have hurt you in the past also; it is safe, will empower you tremendously and allay many fears we might have of starting new relationships that might produce further exes in due course.

Tips On Tapping For Exes:

— We hate people as a direct result of having become hurt in some way. That's natural and normal, and the more they have hurt us, the more we hate them. But there's nothing that binds you as powerfully to the past as hate does.

— Love, on the other hand, sets you free; most of all, unconditional love. If you truly want to be free, grit your teeth and tap a round on just "Stress!" first of all. This will always help improve your energy flow to the point where you can start thinking in terms of the positives you need to overcome that problem.

— There are no reasons or excuses not to take that positive energy approach to any ex, no matter what they did or who they did it to. It takes enormous strength to stand firm and believe in the power of love to transform everything, to heal everything, to evolve everything - but it's worth it in the end.

- Conversely, there is nothing gained at all for tying yourself to the past, no matter how wonderful it was at the time. Time is here and now, and power is here and now. All love can be evolved further. Deep down, you know that too. I believe that our capacity to love is quite literally infinite, and each one of us has only begun to scratch the surface of what's available to each one of us.

Hold a will to love, an intention to love and learning the ways of love above all else. It will give you courage, strength and free your heart.

Finding Love

If you are looking for a partner and haven't found one yet, first of all, and quite literally, TAKE HEART.

I mean that.

Put your hands on your heart of energy and take three deep breaths.

Consider this.

Whatever has gone on before, that's all in the past now.

It really doesn't matter what did or what didn't happen, and for what reasons.

We are here, and now.

We have in EFT alone a method our younger aspects did not have.

Our younger aspects had NOTHING AT ALL to help them with stress, with heartache, to feel better when they needed it. They had no idea that they had energy bodies which needed feeding, care and attention, and neither did all the many people our past aspects interacted with.

No idea at all.

As a result, everything was confusing, beyond confusing. We got very stressed and our aspects thought and did all sorts of things we would never have done at all if we hadn't been so stressed, so desperately low on energy.

We might well have been "looking for love in all the wrong places."

We might even have had completely screwy ideas of what love is and what loving is all about in the first place!

What that means is that what we have may have learned from all of this is of little use to us now.

We've got to start afresh.

Draw a line under what was, take a deep breath and turn the other way, turn to the future, where the new and healing experiences actually exist.

When we change our energy systems by feeding them better, paying more attention to them, getting them to flow better, challenging old blockages afresh, **a different future comes into being.**

It really doesn't matter if you never managed to get anyone to look at you twice before; or if you've had endless successions of partners who made you feel terrible.

The past doesn't matter now.

It's ONLY about the future.

It's ONLY about the future.

It's OK now to fall in love. If it all goes horribly wrong, you can always tap on it and get over it, fast!

I'm not just saying that, I know this to be true through personal experience first of all, but also through having helped hundreds if not thousands of people to "get over it, fast."

It is that knowing which makes all the difference.

The first time I fell in love, it took me fifteen YEARS to get over it. Without EFT or any other form of sensible energy work, that's not surprising. The third to last time it took about a year. The second to last time it happened, it took me a month to get over it. The last time it happened, I didn't get over it at all and instead, found a totally surprising relationship I'm still enjoying as I write this.

What we're doing here isn't some flight of fancy.

It's extremely real, extremely hard hitting and extremely surprising in every way.

With EFT on your side, you can take "emotional risks" - rejection, unrequited love, even betrayal and bereavement won't kill you any longer.

You can do something about it, and no matter how bad it will be, you can get through it, over it, and become stronger in the process.

Indeed, this is what I found the most wonderful in my own explorations of using modern energy work at the deepest personal level - that expectation of experiences, not being afraid of high emotion, not reversing out of potential relationships in fear of what might happen.

To have that knowledge that love won't break you (ever again!) but instead, will enrich you in all manner of ways and help you evolve.

See it was always meant to be that way.

Love was always meant to help us evolve. We just didn't know that, didn't know what to do with it, and became terrified of the power of it.

With that lifted, your future is unknown now, but I can guarantee you that you will be blown away by all those sensations, emotions and experiences you never even dreamed existed.

So with that said, let's get started on the path to find love!

First Steps To Finding Love

When we work with positive energy to make our energy bodies stronger and more shiny, we start with the here and now and stop dwelling on the past.

So the first question I would ask of you is this.

What do you think a relationship will give you that you need to be so much happier?

Look at the positives chart and pick seven positives.

Over the next seven days and nights, tap for one of these positives each per day.

What this does is to take a top level of "neediness" away - it nourishes your energy system with the most needed energy at this time, right here and now and will allow you to breathe more deeply and become far more centred in yourself.

That's the effect of bringing up your energy levels - it makes you calmer, think more clearly, and become happier "in yourself."

I really don't have to tell you how "needy people" are shunned by society or in the dating scene in particular. It's a law of nature that the more you have, the more you get. It seems horribly unfair if you're that desperate sales man who can't sell a thing to anyone, and sells ever less, the more desperate they become; as it seems unfair to a person who is desperate for love and avoided like a leper, but it's a fact.

Being "needy" is not a crime.

It's a result of not having enough love (read "life energy"!) coming your way, it's a result of malnourished energy bodies, of living life, full stop.

It is also not your fault. It's not a character defect.

It's a systemic response to seek more energy when you are low on energy.

What's happened in our societies is that there is this idea that you meet "the one" who will make it all alright and who will fulfil all your energy needs and you'll live happily ever after, but that's not true at all.

It takes a village to raise a child, it takes a village to heal a person, and it takes a village to provide the energy needs of person. A village and a whole world full of skies, weathers, sunshine, animals, plants, rocks, water, air, the stars in the sky ... and a Universe beyond that ...

Even if you haven't found your "the one" just yet, there are endless opportunities to enrich yourself, feed yourself and to essentially stop being needy.

To become strong, happy and shiny.

At which point you're no longer chasing that elusive relationship, and instead, the relationship WILL FIND YOU.

It's structural and inevitable.

So by all means, become aware of what you need. Don't block it out or try and ignore it, don't try to pretend you don't need that or that you're strong in being solitary.

Especially for the gentlemen out there, try and think energy, try and think systemic.

Human beings need tenderness and affection. They need touch and play. They need union, someone to have faith in them, someone to love them.

The positives that you are missing and which you truly hunger for the most are the ones that give you that breakthrough, that turn around in the energy system from "needy" to "shiny and attractive."

Tap on what you need and want from a partner every day, and use the sensation of loneliness and longing to let you know when you can respond by feeding your energy body with more positives.

That's the start, that's the baseline.

When we're ready, it's time to start thinking of what you want in a partner.

From Fantasy To Reality

Everyone has their "dream partner" ideas, and if I've learned one thing over the last fifty years on this planet, they're always dead wrong.

It is hilarious to ask people who are in strong, lasting relationships if they ever dreamed of the kind of person they eventually bonded with.

I can guarantee they'll laugh their heads off and say simultaneously, "No, not in a million years did I dream I was going to find love with (a shoe salesman, an overweight waitress from Idaho, a Greek hippie ...)"

Fantasy lovers get in the way of reality, big time.

It focuses us on the wrong things, mostly on the past, some Guiding Star experience with something or someone a young aspect thought was amazing, be that daddy or a Bond babe from the cinema, the red haired girl singer from that rock band or the hunk from that TV show ...

To unstick yourself when you have become stuck on a certain look, ethnicity, type or temperament, and free yourself up to be able to really see, hear, feel, taste, scent and sense what's out there for you, we can use the following simple pattern to turn a dream lover into finding a real lover.

Focus on your fantasy "perfect partner."

What's so attractive about them?

Make a list. Write down the words carefully, as you would think or speak them, because those words are YOUR WORDS to describe that energy you are attracted to.

"This is my dream lover because he/she is so ..."

In this example, the answers were:

- radiant
- beautiful
- interesting
- forceful
- creative
- sexy
- powerful
- protective
- honest
- unstoppable

So, and instead of asking you to "give up on your dream and accept second best," we're going to ask for exactly those energetic qualities and tap on it:

In the Heart Position:

"I want a partner who is radiant!"

... with the reminder phrase of, "Radiant!" on every point you tap.

What this does is a) give you that radiant energy you crave and b) it expands your concept and experience of "radiant energy."

In other words, it evolves that concept, helps it grow up from where it was first formed, all those many years ago, and brings it into the here-and-now.

This is an excellent example of how instead of berating people for what their heart yearns for, if you can give it to them, they will evolve.

In the end, it's only energy. But it is so personal, and perfect.

A Few Words About You ...

Knowing "who you are" is probably the most powerful thing when it comes to trying to show to others who you are, and finding someone who likes that very much indeed.

We are deeply confused by who we are because we didn't understand how we can be such wonderful people one day, and such stress riddled lunatics the next.

Remember this: You are not showing "your true colours" until you're at least at +5 or above.

Below that, you're light is under the bushel, and you are simply "not yourself."

It doesn't matter at all if you've spent the last 30, 40, 50 years at -5 and thrown yourself around like the proverbial lunatic; that wasn't you being yourself, that was a succession of stressed, harried, starving, parching, desperate aspects.

Put anyone through that sort of thing, and that's what you'll get.

This theoretical musing has everything to do with your self concept, but also quite practically, how you describe yourself in a few words on a dating website, or what you have in your aura if you're walking into a room.

The 1st Rule is therefore:

- **Never even try to figure out who you are or what you can provide for another until and unless you are <u>AT LEAST</u> at a +5 on the energy chart.**

Try this now.

Pick a positive that will lift you to +5 right now, or a progression of positives if you're starting from way back each one of which is specifically chosen to make you "happier," right now.

Now, describe yourself as you would for a dating ad.

Can you tell how different that is? How much truer, more straightforward, more right and attractive that is?

That's getting close to you being yourself.

It's in the right direction.

Remember what this feels like.

This is the you that needs to go shopping for clothes. This is the you that needs to make decisions on your hair style, your music choices, you favourite holiday destinations.

It's not an alien, it's not an altar ego, it's who your genetics, your energetic blueprint (we call it the Creative Template[4]) was originally designed to be.

Getting to know your real self, or at least getting a sense of what it feels like when you're getting a bit closer to your real self, is hugely important.

It's a measurement to let you know when you're starting to get stressed; a goal post in mind, body and spirit you can aim for.

It has also the advantage that once you have more of an idea of who you really are, it becomes highly unlikely that you can "get lost" or "lose yourself" in any relationship, no matter how amazing it might be.

Going Out

Social anxiety - a great cover word for freaking out when in the presence of other people, and especially people who might be potential love partners! - is endemic and systemic.

You would never believe how many people suffer from that, and how many people who seem "the life and soul of the party" have to do all sorts of weird things to be able to seem that way.

Alcohol, drugs, strange rituals of dressing and preparation, medicating yourself and so much more is just the tip of the iceberg.

The first thing I would advise is to make absolutely no distinction between "going out" for a trip to get a pint of milk, or "going out" to a work event, or "going out" on a date.

It's all "going out."

You can practise on every "going out" you do so that when it comes to a date, you are well practised and far more centred in yourself.

---

4   Creative Template from EMO Energy In Motion by Silvia Hartmann DragonRising 2002/2015. Refers to the original blueprint for the energy system that came into being at the moment of conception, is completely individual and the "goal" for energy interventions.

What do you need to be able to go out and feel not just happy in your own skin, but delighted and excited about what you're about to see, hear, feel and experience?

What "super power" could help you have a totally different experience today, for the first time?

"Well, if I was a bit better looking ... "

Give yourself the gift of "Beauty." If you are a gentleman, don't short change yourself to "handsome."

"Beauty" is a hugely powerful positive and something holy, something from the Creative Order itself. It is one of the many names of love, so even if it feels a little strange at first, try that. Tap it mindfully and allow your inbuilt hunger for beauty to awaken.

By all means, do more rounds, "More beauty," and "Beauty in its widest metaphorical sense," and "I am beauty."

Three rounds, then go and buy your pint of milk.

- **What differences are you noticing in the way you experience the world, and how other people are treating you?**

This is the pattern I want you to employ. Don't take my word for it, you need to EXPERIMENT with yourself and the power of the positives to create different experiences.

What you will find is that amongst the many positives you try out and tap on, there are some that have far more instant impact than others.

Finding your own personal power positives that give you an instant lift is of the essence when we go out "in the field" and start doing things with other people for real.

Personal Power Positives

When you are at a party, on a date, at a rock concert or anywhere else out and about in the real world, it can happen that old reversals kick in and you can feel yourself losing the plot, energetically speaking.

Old ticks and trembles might re-emerge, you might start to doubt yourself, lose connection with your power, your intelligence and your radiance; you might feel that old familiar churning in your stomach yet again.

What is very interesting is that when you have tapped a particular positive a few times and it has really helped you feel better, you can simply evoke that positive without having to tap at all.

146

It becomes a trigger for instant energy system changes - a personal power positive or PPP.

Close your eyes just for a moment, take a deep breath and say that positive to yourself in your mind strongly.

You can "breathe in" the positive with the fresh air through your nostrils at the same time.

You will notice a shift, and that is how you make the transition from tapping EFT rounds to a more fluent way of using energy and your energy body to change your state.

Change your state, change your stars.

After The Event

I had an old aunt who always seemed to have a good time at family gatherings, but then would go home and lie in bed awake all night, thinking about all sorts of slights and insults she might or might never have received. She would then "fall out" with people who had no idea what they had done to deserve this, and after a lifetime of this, ended up extremely bitter, twisted, and entirely friendless!

Whatever happened, good or bad, we can review it from a far more positive state and think about what we can do firstly, for the aspect who had those experiences, and for future aspects, to make them even happier and even more successful than they were on this occasion.

If your aspect freaked out completely and lost the plot, that's not a tragedy, it's only feedback. Poor aspect! Perhaps they tried too much, too soon? Perhaps they needed a little more (courage, faith, support, energy) and didn't realise just how stressed they were?

What can we send to a future aspect so they will have a much better experience?

Is there anything practical we can do to support the future aspect on the next excursion?

If you think long term, and treat yourself and all your aspects like you would a youngster under your care, with lots of love, moral support and learning the true lessons of what went on, then you do not need to fear failing once in a while.

Also, and this is important, focus on what the aspect did right or very well.

The aspect might have been very courageous, tried to be creative, had a go.

To give the aspect the credit they deserve is a very loving thing to do, a very empowering thing to do.

And once you've done it a few times, you will notice a strange effect.

Doing something, anything, and knowing that there's no "you" in the future who will be sneering down the timeline at you, and instead of criticising you and calling you a fool and a failure, loves you, understands you and supports you, is an amazing sensation.

Very freeing.

Very empowering.

I do hope you will get to feel this for yourself, and soon!

Long Term Relationships

The best way to enliven and "spice up" long term relationships is to not necessarily send both partners into therapy, or together into couples counselling, but instead, to work on the relationship entity.

- **The relationship entity is the couple bubble which is more than the sum of its parts.**

In any long term relationship, there have been a mountain of incidents, both good and bad, and there exist innumerable if not infinite aspects for each partner.

Working with the relationship entity itself is a very high level intervention, a wonderful short cut and a powerful thing to do.

Have a go and follow along with the steps to get a sense of that.

First of all, think of your relationship, that couple bubble that exists above and beyond you and your partner.

Where is it located when you think about it? Point to it if it outside of you and make a note of its location, how far away, how high, where exactly that is placed in your space.

Some people feel the relationship inside their own bodies; that's fine too, put your hand on that place and pay attention how that feels.

What state is that relationship in? It's an entity, so we can ask, "Is it happy? Blue? Faint? Throbbing?"

How does it appear to you right now? Make a note of that.

Here comes the important question.

"What can we give to this entity, this existence, right now so it becomes much, much happier?"

Let something come to you, and if nothing comes to you, just go for "It needs more love!" as a catch all.

Now, we keep focused on the relationship entity and we'll tap a round of Positive EFT to send it the positive energy it needs to feel happier.

Let the right words come to you or simply tap along with me for now.

Put your hands on your heart and take a deep breath, in and out. Then another, and another. Stay focused on the relationship entity as you start tapping the top of your head and say ...

I send this relationship entity all my love.

I want this relationship entity to be happier and I want this with all my heart!

I send it love and energy from my heart and soul!

I send it love, energy and healing.

Deep ocean waves of love and healing.

I send it love and passion, energy.

Bright fountain energy of love.

Sparkling, delightful energy!

Magical, romantic energy!

Nourishing, wonderful, loving energy ...

Young, bright energy - first love energy!

Extraordinary, beautiful, transformational love energy!

Delightful, creative, sexy love energy!

Powerfully supportive, unconditional love energy!

All the love in the world, a rainbow of energies and beyond!

Strong, powerful, royal, love energy!

Happy laughter energy!

Profound loving energy, heart loving energy ...

All my love.

All my love.

All my love.

How was that?!

Now tune back into the relationship entity and describe out aloud how it has changed to reflect the change at the energy levels that has taken place.

This is a wonderful ... I won't call it an exercise, for it is more than that. It is more than a prayer, more than a spell, it's creating energetic reality and the right thing to do.

More than once, at that ...

Take care of your relationship entity. Be aware of it and treat it with love. Empower it and in so doing, unlock the amazing potential that can be found in long term relationships, to discover new things about yourself and how the relationship can help you transcend yourself with the help of an other.

Loving Yourself

Practically speaking, you cannot love your self any more than you can jump over your own shadow, hear your own voice as it really sounds or see yourself with your own eyes.

Loving any one or any thing is an outward energy movement that has to be directed at someone outside of you.

Think of it in terms of "sending love."

You can send love to past and future aspects of yourself, however, and that's how you can practically love and encourage "yourself."

If there was an aspect in your past who had bad experiences, what can you give/send that aspect now to make it better?

Sending a love gift across time and space is an awesome experience, and it always empowers the sender amazingly - but in this case, it also empowers the recipient. It further makes a connection in the entire energy matrix that may have been disrupted and broken and improves the exchange of information and energy - which makes you wiser, and happier.

Sending positive energy to a future aspect who may face certain challenges also has this tremendous empowering of the person here and now. It's an amazing way to love yourself and **help yourself** to do amazing things in the future. Apart from that, it takes away a whole lot of fear and stress about the future and makes you stronger.

It's highly recommended.

Feeding Yourself

We can send love and positive energy forms to our past and future selves. But what about you and me, right here and now?

Here, think in terms of "feeding yourself."

If you were hungry, and you really loved and cared for this hungry person, what meal would you seek to provide for them?

What does this person, right here and now, need and want to make them happier?

Choose a first positive from the chart, just as you would pick a starter from a restaurant menu.

Indeed, working with energy nutrition and the human energy body is much more closely related to having a good dinner at a restaurant than it is to do with meditation or being all spiritual in some convoluted sense.

What you yearn for, what you are truly hungry for, is exactly what you need to feed to yourself at this moment.

Don't try to be holy or do the pageant princess when you ask yourself what it is that you yearn for above all else. Don't psychoanalyse yourself or try and figure out "what it means about you as a person" that you should be wanting sex, lightning, and power in that order.

It's all just energy, and our energy systems are much, much too complicated to try and explain them and their fluid reactions to the environments and all that's happening moment to moment consciously.

Just keep the list of positives handy and feed yourself freely, easily at any time you feel energetically down or hungry. Your entire mind/body/spirit totality will thank you for it!

And while we're on the restaurant metaphor and before we go - don't forget the cherry on top, and before you're done with your three or five course meal of Michelin starred positives, make sure you order your pudding!

Virtues & Self Esteem

Psychotherapy approaches have been focusing exclusively on "what's wrong with me, and who's to blame for that" in spirit for a long time.

There is no definitive answer to that question; indeed, these sort of questions **generate infinite answers** simply by virtue of asking them.

We can use that same method of generating infinite, never ending answers the other way around when we are looking to work with love, rather than with negativity.

So we can ask, "What's right about me, and who takes the praise for that?"

One of the finest "self esteem boosters" I know is to ask a person what they are good at, what virtues, talents, skills or natural abilities they know they have - and then to tap on that.

It is fascinating how this can affect a person and how much good that does.

For example, a lady said that she was a "good listener."

She tapped on that set up and had a big breakthrough moment when she understood that it wasn't just about listening at all, it was about being present, opening your heart to a person, and giving love back. In other words, a very powerful, actively loving endeavour rather than a passive thing as she had always previously imagined.

Just this one round of EFT on one good quality had a huge impact on this lady and opened the door for a real evolution in how to relate to other people - and how to assess her own value and worth, at that.

Another lady who was very creative had a revelation during a round of Positive EFT for creativity - she became very excited at the idea of applying the same processes of creativity she employed in her paintings in her love life! She said, "I just can't believe that I had that so compartmentalised - it was like my creativity was boxed up and only came out in the studio." Then she laughed and added, "You should have seen my partner's face when I became very creative for the first time ... He was so amazed and inspired by it, our relationship is on a whole new level now."

And there was a gentleman who prided himself on his logical engineering mind who discovered to his amazement that understanding his wife was also a matter of logic - she was actually very predictable and there was "a logical way to make her happy." He was amazed by that and I was delighted, as one of my all time favourite quotes is, "Love without logic is insanity - and vice versa."

An End To Self Punishment

A huge part of "learning to love yourself right" is to recognise any forms of self-berating, self-mutilating, self-punishment as simply signs of a stressed person who is low on essential life giving energy and needs a positive boost.

At the energy levels it is true that "punishment creates crime."

If any aspect of you has done something you consider to be bad or wrong, has made a mistake you now regret, made bad decisions or messed up in any shape or form, take a deep breath first of all.

Then, consider what this aspect might need so this won't ever happen again.

What does this aspect need to evolve?

Does it need more intelligence? Kindness? Energy? Love? Patience?

Tap on those and note what that does to you, right here and now; to your feelings towards the aspect in question; and about your assessment of how that will affect your future.

If you really seriously want to become "a better person" then getting rid of punishment, emotional, physical or intellectual abuse of not just yourself now, but all aspects, past, present and future, is the way forward.

Love, pure energy by any other name, is the answer.

This doesn't mean that we'll be perfect and flawless all the time.

It just means that we spend less time in the low energy states, and recover much more quickly - that our average improves with age, in other words.

We all have our moments.

Understanding that the solution is to send more love and support, not less, is the most important step in the right direction to a happier, more productive and of course, more love filled life you can take.

An End To Martyrdom

This headline refers to "how to love yourself inside a relationship."

And not to do this is by making yourself miserable in order to please the other.

When you really love someone, of course you want to make them happy, serve them in any way possible, and do your very best for them.

When does doing your best to make the other person happy turn into martyrdom?

When you stop enjoying it and it becomes painful, hard, or a chore. When it starts making you unhappy.

Then you must stop and find a different way.

For almost every problem, and perhaps indeed for every problem there is, there are creative solutions that can make both partners happy.

Don't look for "compromise."

Compromise is when both of you end up being unhappy and dissatisfied.

Look for a win-win where both end up ecstatically happy and don't stop seeking such a solution, such a victory.

What would it take for you to be able to start doing (x) or stop doing (x) so you can be happier more often and miserable less often?

The first stop tap for some situations is the positive of "It would take a miracle!"

Especially where people and their ways, their behaviours, their emotions are concerned, we keep thinking that nothing can be done, because we all come from a world where indeed, nothing COULD be done - because we were working without energy in mind!

Just with EFT alone, there are literally infinite ways to change any situation, no matter how old, stuck or severe it may appear.

It's only energy!

A simple example is a wife martyring herself by going fishing with her husband when she hates fishing but loves the husband and his company. However, and especially if it rains and is cold and windy, she gets ever more miserable and hates it more and more.

Yet she continues to go - that's martyrdom.

We can approach this - what is in essence a non-problem and just some kind of major energy blockage - in many different ways.

We could ask, what positive energy form does the suffering aspect who is cold, miserable and hates her life on that last fishing trip need? What can we give her? Faith, trust, confidence, a miracle?

After a few positives, this example person started to laugh and called out, "She needs better wet weather gear!"

What about the aspect who hates slimy wet fish and the smell of them?

The answer that came, especially after the wet weather gear breakthrough, "She needs to lighten up! She needs lightness, energy, love!"

At some point, there comes a breakthrough. This can be the realisation that the relationship is strong enough so she doesn't need to go fishing every time, or at all. It could have been that the wet weather occurrences are rare, and many wonderful, intimate experiences were had in beautiful nature settings, so the odd getting wet and cold wasn't a high price to pay after all.

It could even be that if it is cold and miserable, she stays at home and goes along when the sun is shining.

These and a myriad other ways and means to be happier and get what you want out of life present themselves readily once we're through that misery barrier and into thinking truly positive.

There is no need for martyrdom, and that's a big step forward in learning to "love yourself" in a whole new way.

Your Pursuit Of Happiness

The energy chart shows us that if you want to be a better person, the only way you're going to get there is by being much, much happier, much, much more often.

That's not the way we were taught or brought up, and it's a complete reversal to how we tend to think by default.

Your happiness is your measurement device as to how well you are doing with your relationship, with your work, with your life.

Your happiness doesn't come "after" or "second best" to your family, your children, or your partners.

To give your family, your children and your partners the "best you" you can possibly be, you need to be the happiest you can possibly be.

"Happy" as in at least on the right side of the energy chart makes you more patient, more loving, more powerful and more useful to absolutely everyone in your life.

It doesn't make you into some crazy person who is running around laughing like a lunatic all the time.

It makes you into a very stable, centred person who has lots of love, attention and moral support to give.

The more you have,
the more you have to give.

You have it in your hands - in the case of EFT, quite literally! - to make yourself and all your aspects a whole lot happier.

Go for that.

Pursue your own happiness.

That's how we learn to "love ourselves."

And remember!

Your happiness MATTERS.

Romance

What is "romance"?

I had the great good fortune to have been the tapping partner for a young lady who chose "romance" as her positive - I would never have thought of tapping for this.

I learned many things in the course of that one single round which left both of us absolutely delighted, laughing and hugging (we had only just met, at a Mind/Body/Spirit exhibition stand where we were offering free Positive EFT demonstrations).

I learned that being romantic is something for both men and women in equal measure (before that, I had expected men to bring romance to me, rather than the other way around, and I never knew that!);

I learned that romance is being aware of the potential in the moment for romance - you don't have to wait until Valentine's Day, when there is a will to be romantic, you can have it any time;

I learned that romance is a wonderful thing, light and playful, and that it should occur every day in an ongoing relationship.

Most of all, I learned that romance is nothing mysterious. It's just being loving when the moment presents itself.

And that happens simply a lot more often when you are happy from the energy system up, not stressed, not distracted.

Words of romance also follow naturally when you are in a high energy state. You don't have to learn them, they just come to you and are light and easy.

Romance is a wonderful thing. It's a wonderful positive. Let more romance into your life, no matter who you are. It won't make you weak; but it might just bring you star moments of happiness you will remember to your dying day.

I want more romance in my life.
More romance in its widest metaphorical sense.
All the romance in the Universe!
Romantic days, romantic nights ...
Moments of life changing romance ...
Beautiful romance ...
Soul inspiring romance ...
Heart expanding romance ...
Sexual romance ...
Physical romance ...
Feeling romance in every cell of my body ...
I am romance!

Sexual Energy

Tapping SEX as a positive does a number of the most amazing things.

Firstly, to consider it as a positive energy form, in and of itself, is to many people who have been stuffed up with shame and guilt a major revelation.

In modern energy work, when we say SEX we don't mean shagging, we mean the energy of sex, sexual energy, and energy exchanges that happen between people before, during and after sex.

And what we now call 1st Circuitry energy is absolutely the most powerful energy flows in the energy body.

If you want "power for life" and really activate yourself, transform yourself, here is the main power line that goes straight through the middle of your energy body and will set your incarnation on fire, if you let it.

The main power line of the 1st Circuitry runs straight through the heart of energy too and contrary to public opinion, actually empowers the heart.

Conversely, when the 1st Circuitry is choked off and blocked up, the heart suffers from chronic undernourishment.

And that creates weird symptoms in mind, body and spirit across the board.

Which is why Dr Freud came to the conclusion that just about everything that is wrong with people has to do with repressed sexuality!

If he had made that leap to repressed (or de-pressed!) sexual ENERGY, he would have been right on the money.

Putting some energy through the 1st Circuitry, simply to raise the energy levels and charge the heart of energy and for no other reason than that is the absolute fast track to a healthy energy body.

- **SEX is a positive energy.**

Take a deep breath, take heart - literally! - assume the Heart Position, focus on sex in terms of sexual energy (Where do you feel that in your body? Pay attention!) and tap a slow, thoughtful round of Positive EFT with the evocation of SEX.

It's an extraordinary thing.

There will be flashing thoughts, strange body sensations as old blocked energy starts to move at long last, and all sorts of sensations you may have never felt before.

Focus on the sensations and on the energy flow. We are dealing "only" with energy here, and once you start to warm up and come to life, you can another round and make it known what kind of sexual energies you want more of in your life.

Safe sex. Happy sex. Joyful sex. Innocent sex. Wonderful sex. Enlightening sex. Transformational sex. Lightning sex. Powerful sex. Holy sex. The choice is yours!

There is nothing that lights up an adult human energy system like 1st Circuitry energy and once you have flushed out a few of your blockages on the topic, you can use sexual energy in daily life at any time you need a really strong boost through your daily endeavours.

Feeling miserable? Blue? Cold? Depressed? Tired? Hopeless? Sexy energy will put pay to that in minutes, often even faster than that.

There is a reason why so many people look at porn sneakily during their working day, or do some "sexting" with other people. They are using that sexual energy to boost whatever else it is they are doing - but often with a lot of shame and guilt attached, for "porn energy" isn't clean and clear and brings its own problems over time.

By freeing the idea of sexual energy from the material world in essence and having it be what it was always meant to be, namely energy FOR LIFE ITSELF once again, you unlock a veritable powerhouse of an energy system.

And don't be afraid. The higher you get on the energy scale, the more intelligent, far sighted, better protected and more loving you become. You will also become more beautiful, more radiant and things such as self confidence, body confidence and so forth resolve themselves and cease to be an issue.

Learning to understand your own sexual energy flows, your very own 1st Circuitry, can make a HUGE difference to every aspect of your life.

For many, many people, it is indeed that key to unlocking their own power they have been looking for all along.

Sexual energy.
Empowering sexual energy.
Rejuvenating sexual energy.
Light, powerful, rushing sexual energy.
Sexual energy bringing my body to life.
Empowering sexual energy.
Life saving sexual energy.
Life giving sexual energy.
Uplifting sexual energy
Glorious sexual energy.
God given sexual energy.
Enlightening sexual energy.
Transformational sexual energy.
I am powerful, strong and alive!

The Sex Journey

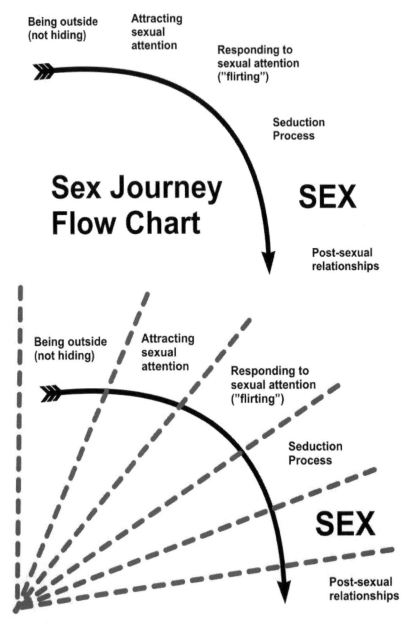

The diagram on top is the complete sexual journey, and the one beneath shows the threshold breaks.

The first one is "not hiding." That's when people come out of their caves and start hesitantly looking around or going out. If the break is before that step, you have your general recluse. They might go out to work but they're hiding behind shields and clothing so they are not a target for attention.

Next is the break before flirting.

So we have people going out and actively inviting attention, but when someone gives it, they freak out and run home and that's where the journey ends for them.

After flirting comes seduction. Contrary to popular opinion, it's game played by two with each other. That's the mating dance when both parties have decided sex will be had and are getting ready to be doing that, getting in sync.

If the break is at this point, you get serial seducers and prick teasers. They'll have a very difficult time with relationships because to go that far and then not have sex is going to make the other party very angry and confused.

Next is sex itself. If the break comes here, then we have people who have a lot of sex but kick their partners out in the morning, or conversely sneak off and won't take your phone calls.

Finally, there's the post-sexual relationship. Could be sex buddies, could be marriage, could be just good friends. Could even be saying goodbye with a kiss after breakfast and "Thank you, you've enriched my life, I will never forget you ..." aka an active relationship resolution that in and of itself is also a relationship.

The reason I made this is to demonstrate there is only one journey with these different evolutionary stages which makes it wrongfully appear as though there is this totally confusing mess of difference.

To make the very important note that the people on the other side of one of the red dividing marks will find every reason in the book as to why it is not just the right thing, but the ONLY thing to be doing what they're doing.

And not just that, that all the people who are doing other things are clearly crazy or sex mad or immoral or just downright WRONG full stop.

Which accounts for the confusion.

Each one of the red lines represents a threshold, and what is needed is enough energy to take a person through that threshold and onto the other side, on to the next step.

This does not only apply to single people, but the Sex Journey is taken in relationships too, every time AFRESH.

In theory, every single time this Sex Journey completes, an evolution should have taken place in the energy system.

In theory, every time a person takes this journey, they should be on an uplifting spiral that gets better and better with age and experience.

In theory, as I said ... :-)

You can use this diagram to spot where you have run up across a barrier, an energy blockage that stops you from going further, or that precludes successfully moving on to the next step, and then eventually, onto the next level.

Where are your sticking points, and what energy is needed to free you up to have more, new and better experiences?

- **What energy do you need to stop hiding?**
- **What energy do you need to attract more attention?**
- **What energy do you need to handle others being strongly attracted to you?**
- **What energy do you need to start flirting, to elegantly engage in the "mating dance"?**
- **What energy do you need to have safe and wonderful sex?**
- **And what energy do you need to have a wonderful post-sexual relationship?**

Every person who has sex or who wants to have sex can use empowering energy form to get HIGHER. Wherever you are, there's more. There's always another step, another unfoldment, and this being so, there can be no competition.

We all have so much to learn, so much to explore!

Enjoy the process, and know that for the fully actualised human energy body, the Sex Journey is absolutely the fast track to enlightenment.

Sex With A Partner

First of all, let us remember that no matter how wonderful you already are as a sex partner, there is always room for evolution.

This being so, and all of us needing and wanting to evolve, whether we know this or not, we're all in the same boat.

It doesn't matter if you have had a thousand sexual partners or none at all; if you've been with that special person for a week, a year, a decade or a century.

Every single time we engage in the sexual journey, it is new, different (because you are different, you are not the same aspect you were yesterday and neither is your partner!), and it presents a major opportunity for personal evolution.

When we work with Positive EFT, we don't go into the reasons for why some things aren't working as they should, or why some things don't feel right or are totally out of reach.

We go for the energetic solutions to the energy blockages that hold us back.

As this is so personal and so different for each and every person, let's make it simple and ask first of all,

"What do I need right now to take me to the next level?"

Take a look at the basic list of positives.

Let something jump out at you and tap for that.

Then ask, "What else do I need?" - and tap for that.

You can think of these positives as a form of energetic Viagra, and the reason I am mentioning this is that energy work, when it's done right, is as reliable as any chemical; indeed more so as you don't get any evil side effects.

You can also proxy tap for your partner - what does she/he need to take this to the next level?

We can also address then the "couple" as a separate entity that is more than the sum of their parts in every way - what does this couple need to take this to the next level?

This is a wonderful thing to do; and it gets even better still if you and your partner can do this together.

When you tap together on the "couple entity," you are not trying to make each other better, or be each other's therapist - that is so important in a partnership which has to be a union of equals to work as it should.

You don't have to argue whose fault anything is, you don't have to blame anything on anyone, you can just say, "What do we want for this couple? What would make them even happier still?"

Perhaps more lightness? More fun? More inspiration? More creativity? More sexiness? More excitement?

Take turns to give these **gifts** to the couple as you tap together and note how the energy builds up between you, how rapport deepens as you breathe together and align your intention for the relationship itself.

It's a wonderful experience.

With partners who won't tap, you can just hold hands and come up with blessings for the relationship instead; of course there is more to playing with energy than just tapping!

And this brings me to paying more attention to the energy of sex with a partner through all its stages.

Become more aware of where energy is lost, where you or your partner are losing power and sliding away and down on the energy chart.

Make a mental note and help these power-outages formulate your plan for future improvements.

Bringing energy awareness into the physical relationship is a gift of unbelievable proportions and a gift that keeps on giving.

The more energy aware we become, the more opportunities we are able to perceive to have new, different, amazing experiences with and through each other.

When touch becomes electric, breath taking, or a kiss shudders through your entire body as though you were struck by lightning, we are really talking about whole body experiences on a totally different level.

Allow yourself to want that, to expand that, to discover just how much better than you ever thought you can feel, with all your heart.

We were built for pleasure, not for suffering.

We are radiant beings encased in a living skin that can create the greatest symphonies of sensations, new and afresh each time.

This is truly transformational stuff, and the most exciting journey there could be.

Oh - and it gets ever better with age ... ☺

Social Anxiety

Social anxiety is amazingly, absolutely rampant and much, much more common than you might ever imagine.

If you go out to any kind of congregation of people, be it to church on a Sunday, a pop concert, a football game, a family birthday party, a club or a pub, a house party and simply stand in a corner and look out for "the signs of stress" in people - my oh my ...

Social anxiety is massively masked with all manner of addictions, repetitive behaviours, rituals and stimulants.

Why does the very idea of having to go out and meet people cause us so much stress?

Well, that's the old way of asking, isn't it.

This leads us into a myriad reasons and into the past, when we want to concern ourselves strictly with the now, and the future.

Have a look at the SUE scale - where would you say you would find yourself if you were to enter a room full of strangers by yourself?

When would you start to worry about it, and how low can your energy flow go?

To overcome social anxiety, by any other name, we need to do ... what?

Of course.

We need to bring our energy systems up to the positive side of the energy chart, and get it up as high as possible, and keep it there.

Therefore, what we need is

a) a set of positives that will empower us before the event, in the run up to the event;

b) a set of positives as we enter into the event;

c) and a set of positives we can use after the event to get ready for the next event.

So let us start with a) and at the beginning.

Think of a social event you will be attending in the coming month. If there's no such event, decide to go for a visit to your local bar in a months' time and use this to check how your energy system reacts to this idea.

How are you feeling in yourself?

Take a moment and a deep breath to become aware of any tension, tightness, uneasiness, or any other signs that you're not entirely happy.

Take another deep breath and ask yourself, "What positive can I tap to make me feel better about this?"

Take a look at the chart and pick your first positive.

Tap the round of EFT and when you're done, think about the event again, and notice what feels different now. Also notice how your thinking about attending the event has changed.

What do you need next, to make you even more relaxed? What would you need to actually start looking forward (!) to the event?

Pick a positive and tap that.

Keep picking positives to tap until you can really begin to feel a sense of excitement in your body about the possibilities and the potential of having new experiences at this event.

Actually allow yourself to really look forward to this event.

By all means, test yourself. What if it all goes horribly wrong and it's all a terrible disappointment? What positive would you need to be able to handle that, to get over it, to laugh it off?

Find the right positive for you and tap on it.

By all means, keep going until you are happy and fully satisfied with your results.

I would make the note that "curing social anxiety" is not a one time deal. Indeed, I don't even want you to think of it like that.

What I'd like you to think instead is, "How can I keep my energy body happy?"

That's a daily and nightly thing to consider, and the more you do that, the better you get at it.

When it then comes to more stressful situations, such as social gatherings, you know what to do and how to do it.

Energy Boosts "In The Field"

One of the things people worry about is what might happen at the event, or "in the field" as the term goes, when and if it all goes horribly wrong. As it did so many times before ...

Take heart, my friend!

Quite literally, take heart.

The "many times before," that was a totally different aspect.

That was an aspect who had not yet read this book, had not yet realised how the energy system regulates whether we're an angel or a fool, and had not yet started to do some basic Positive EFT to feel better, fast.

The aspects for whom it all went horribly wrong also did not understand how other people are ALSO very stressed in social situations, and thereby are often not themselves, either.

What these other people's aspects did and said, might well not reflect any truth - they were just stressed, scared, low of energy and probably drunk as well.

When you start "thinking energy," the whole game changes.

Everything is different, and everything is new.

I want you to take your time and go out there in safety, observing the effects of energy, the energy exchanges that take place between people, and become simply amazed at how different the whole world becomes.

How much more potential for all manner of interesting experiences and experiments comes into being. It's absolutely fascinating to play with people and with energy!

Now here are a few short tips on how to survive energy emergencies in the field.

1. Pay attention to yourself and your energy states! If you have to, leave the room every ten minutes or so, stand outside, take a deep breath and wonder just how amazing you think you are at this time. This will give you a measurement on the amount of stress you are experiencing. If it's pretty bad, you need to take some action right away!

2. You can creep off to the toilet or into the car park, find a spot where you are unobserved and start tapping some Positive EFT. Many have done this and it works a treat! Nobody will notice either, they're all far too stressed to pay much attention, so don't worry about it and do something for your energy system as and when you need it.

3. For long term use, I highly recommend that you find one particular positive that jives with you especially, that always lifts you and gives you excellent electric full body sensations, every time you employ it. Practise tapping this on a regular basis, and then it becomes an anchor and you just have to think or say that positive to yourself ("evoke the positive") to get a noticeable lift in the moment, and without tapping.

4. If you really get stressed or distressed, LEAVE. Taking care of your energy body is the first order of the day, and preventing a meltdown is the sensible thing to do. When you get home, you can tap for the aspect who became overwhelmed and send them love and support through time and space. You can also take the opportunity to send some powerful positives to future aspects in similar situations.

5. Rome wasn't built in a day, and truly, this is about much more than just "overcoming social anxiety." That's just the first step, the real love journey lies on the other side of that threshold. If you keep at it and focus on making your energy body as powerful and as happy as you can, you will make progress and you will get excellent results. I promise!

Soul Mate

The truth is that nobody really knows anything about our mysterious souls that can be proven or reliably explained; souls are pretty inexplicable.

I personally believe that we have systems in our energy body which are not tied to or correlating to physical systems; that this system is "the soul," and that the soul is the wellspring of what we might call magic in this life.

I also believe that the soul really needs to evolve, to grow and get ready so it doesn't fall apart when the physical body dies, and that soul matters are of the essence if we want to unlock the possibility of life after death.

The following ideas are only my personal opinions which I offer for your consideration. There are things I know and I am sure of, and many of those I have written about in this book.

About the soul ... who is to say?

Who can possibly claim to be an authority?

So with these disclaimers, here we go!

I believe that each person has their own soul, and that this soul is unique and has its own unique path of unfoldment.

I do not believe that anyone shares a soul with anyone else, or that there are two people walking around who have only one soul.

I do appreciate that it can feel like that, that one can have a connection that is so strong with another human being that we are dissolving in a *couple bubble*, an extended energy system which contains two people but feels like only one; but at the end of the day, and whether they know this or not, it's one soul per person.

I hold the concept of there being only one soul mate available to every one of us as extremely dangerous and potentially very damaging.

I call it the "the one" delusion.

The idea that there is a "the one" out there who will ...

... make everything alright;

... will make you immortal;

... will take all your pain and fear away;

... will love you unconditionally and forever;

... is the ultimate solution to all your worldly and unworldly problems.

I think this is a misconception and a misdirection; I think that this "the one" people are seeking is in fact their own soul.

That's the only thing which can provide all of that; to ask another human being of flesh and bone to provide all of that is ... an impossible ask.

I further believe that in the mistaken quest for "the one" in flesh form, people are a) getting further and further away from their own souls, and b) in the meantime, missing out on the endless opportunities to evolve offered by "the many" who are all around us.

I have made the comment earlier that it takes a village to raise a child, it takes a village to heal a person, and it takes a village to provide any single human being with all the love they need to thrive.

By endlessly questing for only "the one," a narrow stress focus comes into being and all the other opportunities for love and evolution are overlooked.

So I take the following stance.

"The one" is our own soul. Which we have, we don't need to seek it. We become more aware of its presence and what it is when our energy states become higher, finer and lighter. That's when we get closer to the realms where our own souls live and we can then flow energy and information from and to our soul - which is always most fascinating.

There are lots and lots of other souls, and every one has a person who is attached to it. In principle, every soul and every person offers us the opportunity to evolve, we might just need to become aware of that and actively pay attention, ask the question, "How can you help me evolve?"

The answers are likewise, fascinating.

Every so often, we meet a person with whom we click, big time. They set our energy systems alight for whatever reason, and if it wasn't for all the shields, barriers and disturbances we all have in our systems, amazing things could happen.

Alas, usually our energy systems, totally unused to high energy flows and hardly holding together as they are, tend to go into some form of meltdown when that happens, and we go "love crazy."

We really and honestly feel that we must die if we don't get to have that person, and find all manner of reasons to support those feelings and opinions. The idea that there is only one single "the one," and this person is "it," is a part of that.

When it doesn't work out with this person, they leave or die or don't even want anything to do with us at all, we are heart broken. "This was the one, I didn't get her/him, I'll never find love now ..."

It sounds reasonable, but the fact is that every single person who has tapped EFT on such a thing came out of it with, "Yes, I loved them, but I have so much love to give, I will find a new love!"

"The one" turns out to have been "**the first one**."

There are more to come, and each one is more amazing than the next.

I appreciate that there will be those who are truly appalled at that statement, but likewise, I truly believe that there are many souls, many lives, and we're not on this Earth to suffer.

We need to love lots and lots, never get stuck in love.

Finding a partner who really works with us, who loves us back, is a wonderful thing. I strongly believe that if your soul doesn't want you to be with someone, then you simply would not be.

Souls are funny things and their ways are truly, mysterious.

It is perfectly possible that souls get together behind people's backs and make a plan of their own; and this may involve sharing a time on the journey together. It's a wonderful thing when that happens and when it works.

I do however think that to have only one soul mate and to spend the rest of life in a state of lovelessness and regret CANNOT BE anything other than an energy blockage, a reversal, a major misunderstanding.

The world is so abundant with people, with energy, with life and love, it doesn't make any sense that soul mates should be in such short supply.

But having said all of that, if you truly believe you have found your "the only one, ever, in all times spent" soul mate, go with your own feelings, go with your heart.

Send your soul mate positive energy and use Positive EFT to love them even more. It has been my experience that eventually, there is a breakthrough into enormous clarity, and an evolution towards unconditional love.

And a really wonderful, safe and forward moving thing to do is to also seek a more intimate connection with your own soul.

What positive energy would help you get closer to your own soul?

Pick something.

Start tapping ...

I want to get closer to my soul.

I want to understand my soul.

I want to improve the energy flow between me and my soul.

My soul is precious!

I love my soul - and my soul loves me.

I am the embodiment of my soul.

My soul shines from within me.

I evoke the true power of my soul.

My immortal soul.

My beautiful, beautiful soul.

My mysterious, wonderful, magical soul.

I love my soul!

Unrequited Love & Obsession

It is a most peculiar occurrence that one person can fall head over heels in love with another, and that other is entirely unmoved by this, doesn't notice, and doesn't love them back.

It is probably the most unfortunate of situations a person can find themselves in, and it can lead to all sorts of unfortunate states of being and behaviour.

Have you ever obsessed over anyone, stalked anyone?

Perhaps you are the type of person who instead, becomes the target of the obsessing and the stalking?

Either way, the key to getting control over your emotions, over your love life and your future is to understand that there is something happening INSIDE OF YOU that may have been triggered by that other person, but which belongs to you, and belongs to you alone.

You own that, all of that.

Something has happened in **your** energy system, and this is something important, amazing.

In fact, your energy system was trying to have a full on enlightenment experience.

A huge amount of energy rushed through the system, but that system wasn't ready to take it.

You can think of it as having a starship that begins to shake itself apart as it nears light speed.

That is why there is such a trail of destruction for the person to whom that love strike has happened, and why it feels so confusing, so overwhelming, so painful.

The reason for obsession with another person, regardless of whether they love back or not, or don't even exist at all, as happens in the case of someone falling in love with the illusion of a pop star or a movie star, for example, is that just like in a phobia, the trigger got linked to the experience.

We call the opposite of a trauma a Guiding Star.[5]

---

5   Guiding Stars and other energy system events are explained in "Events Psychology" by Silvia Hartmann, DragonRising 2009/2014

All and everything that was in the environment at the moment when that explosion in the energy system happened becomes linked to that experience, and if the attempted threshold shift in the energy system doesn't complete properly, we literally get stuck there.

It is exactly the same system which causes a PTSD sufferer to experience flash backs to the moment they stepped on the grenade which causes Guiding Star sufferers to get stuck in that "love."

It really isn't their fault, and until 2002, nobody even knew that this was a major problem and a huge missing field from psychology.

Guiding Stars - moments of high positive energy discharge - directly cause the formation of addictions, obsessions, collections, fetishes and philias of all kinds and being stuck on a Guiding Star does more damage in the long run to an incarnation than the worst of trauma ever could.

At least trauma sufferers know what happened and can try to avoid their triggers; Guiding Star sufferers truly believe that their particular thing is the answer to their problems and cannot get away from them.

They don't want to get away from them.

The object of desire is the only thing that ever made them feel that good, and it is structurally immaterial whether that object of desire is a shoe, a Star Wars toy, the singer in a band on TV, or that person they have "fallen in love with."

It is Guiding Stars that keep people stuck in abusive relationships, not their low self esteem, and this fact is simply unknown by either the professional or the pop psychology community.

We may consider that all "falling in love" with anything at all is in essence, a Guiding Star. This is not the case. When the lightning strike of falling in love with someone or some thing happens, and it rushes through the system cleanly, there is no formation of an addiction or obsession.

In the contrary. One feels absolutely free and "enlightened" by the experience, delighted, and one uses the experience as a springboard into a new future.

Guiding Stars, on the other hand, loop us right back into the past in a most powerful way.

But there's a reason for why it's called a GUIDING star.

There is an evolution trying to happen which was not completed at the time, could not be completed at the time, because the energy system wasn't ready or there was structural damage and blockages which caused it to misfire.

- **When we evolve a Guiding Star, we set free absolutely enormous power in the energy system and complete that transformation that's been trying to complete itself ever since it happened.**

By drawing our attention over and over again to the object of desire, the trigger from the Guiding star, our energy system is trying to tell us, "That's what you need to evolve! That's where you are stuck! DO SOMETHING ABOUT THIS!"

In the past, people have tried to "break that obsession" with will power or with punishment; this leads to some dreadful repercussions, as it would.

Mis-treating a Guiding Star can lead to nervous breakdowns, insanity, severe psychosomatic illness and death.

What you need to know about getting free of Guiding Stars is that you need more love, not less.

More love.

More energy.

Enough of the right kind of energy so that the transformation which was trying to happen back then and has been stuck and looping ever since will actually finally happen, and that person is set free once more.

We have already addressed how to switch from "that person" (or "that object") to considering the energy of the situation, and this pattern applies here as well.

If you are obsessing about another person or are caught in the loop of unrequited love, consider the object of your attraction *energetically*.

What is it that they have that you need?

Make a list about everything that is so "attractive" to you, that you need so badly that you think that by possessing this person, it will complete you?

The amazing thing is that no matter how deluded an obsessive, a love lorn or a stalker may seem to everyone around them, they really do need certain energy forms to evolve them.

It's completely true and right, and that drive to somehow "possess" the other person is born from that.

Only, you can't get that energy by abducting the person and chaining them up in your cellar. You can't even get it by convincing them to marry you. They still have that energy, and you still don't.

Energy forms are not tied to a person at all, and by "feeding yourself" with energy (rather than cooking and eating your victims!) you are doing the right thing.

Don't be afraid that you will love less.

You'll love more, better, more deeply by far.

And you will have evolved, which is truly of the essence.

So this is the pattern.

First of all, start with you, right here and now.

- **What do you need above all else to feel more stable, more powerful, more radiant, less stressed?**

Take your time and tap the positives which attract you so that you are in a good state before you consider the next step. As always, you can start with, "Well that would take a MIRACLE ..." as the first positive and then work from there, picking more and different positives as you get into the swing of things.

When you feel strong, happy, and ready to go, we can take the next step, and this will be easy from +5 or above.

Gaze across space and time to tune in on the aspect who had that original experience of falling in love.

Connect with that aspect (but do not become that aspect!) and send the aspect energy gifts across time and space.

Keep with the question of, "What does that aspect need to be able to love _**even more**_?"

Always remember the base principle - MORE love is the answer, more energy, not less, that will make it worse.

With Guiding Stars that have had particularly dire consequences, we may feel that the aspects involved did terrible things, or that need to forgive the aspects first and before we can send them love.

Forgiveness is a state that happens after we have healed our significant energetic injuries. You get forgiveness free of charge after the healing has happened.

The healing itself happens through giving more love - finding positives which are all aspects of love. Giving more and more love until eventually the threshold shift occurs and we break through into this extraordinary space of freedom, clarity and beauty in mind, body and spirit.

When we have evolved the original aspect who had the Guiding Star experience, a logical path forward and what to do next comes into being. It may involve sending love and energy to the object of attraction too, and others who have been drawn into the vortex along the way.

It is extraordinary to think that something as basic and simple as adding more love and energy can produce results in circumstances where nothing else will work at all.

Working with our energy systems in matters of the heart is breathtaking in its simplicity and effectiveness.

It's astonishing.

It needs to be known about, much further and wider because it avoids so much suffering, I can not even find words for it.

Here's the progression once more in brief.

1) Start by empowering yourself so you are at least a +5 on the energy chart. If necessary, start with, "I need a MIRACLE today ..." and tap the first round for miracle as a positive.

2) Tap as many positives as you need so you feel strong and not only ready to create a major shift in evolution for yourself and a healing event, but you're literally rearing to go.

3) When you're ready, gaze across space and time to the aspect who fell in love, at the moment that happened. Take a moment to become aware of just what happened there, the energy movements in that aspect's body. Really pay attention to the point where you can sense what the aspect was feeling; that's called "tuning in" and establishes the energetic connection between you and the aspect.

4) Now send that aspect more love - what energy does this aspect need to finally evolve beyond that place they've been stuck in for so long? If in doubt, simply send love, more love, and all the love in the universe.

5) You will feel in your own body when that threshold shift occurs. You'll get a rush of additional information (energy!) and you will know something amazing has just happened.

This is the basic pattern to deal with any aspect you want to evolve, who is stuck somewhere, and evolving aspects who got stuck on a seemingly good event is probably the most evolutionary energy work we can do at this time, so give it a go!

Stalkers

I have worked with many people who had stalkers and I am extremely aware of how scary and miserable life becomes when you are the object of attraction for a person who had a near miss enlightenment experience and is now completely convinced that you are "*the one* ..."

"The one" and "the ONLY one" who has the power to save their entire incarnation ...

The automatic reaction, the one we have been taught and practised, and which has been practised upon us, courtesy of societal conventions on how to raise children right, is to put up shields and barriers to the stalker.

This reduces the energy flow from you to them and if you remember the "attention seeking escalation" will make them more desperate, and escalate their behaviours, sometimes to a dangerous level.

The easiest and simplest way to make a stalker stop stalking and move along on their life's journey is to apply the basic relationships pattern to the situation.

Again, the automatic reaction, entrained to the core, is to cry, "No! No!!! I don't want anything to do with them! I have no relationship with them and I don't want one!"

The principle that you need more love (energy) to solve problems, not less, **is a law of nature**.

This being so, there are no exceptions to that rule.

None.

Not one.

It is always true.

If you are the victim of a stalker, you need to first of all and above all else, empower yourself correctly in the context of this relationship.

Many stalkees say that they don't understand how the stalker can make them feel so powerless, when they are normally well grounded and happy individuals. It's only in the relationship with the stalker that they become weak, feeble and terrified.

So, and after having de-stressed yourself in the here and now by tapping Positive EFT on a some desirable energies to get you to the point where you can tackle this relationship mess at the energetic levels, tune in on the aspect of you that is the terrified stalkee.

What does he or she need, right now, to not be so terrified any longer?

Send them this, urgently, and pay attention to what happens when you do, to the aspect, to you, how you feel about that aspect.

Continue to empower the stalkee until there is a definite threshold shift and you can really feel a sense of release and lifting.

Only when this has happened, do we turn our attention to the stalker.

Tune in on the aspect of the stalker who had the Guiding Star that made them "get stuck on you."

What does he/she need to evolve, urgently?

Send them this. The more you can help them evolve, the faster everyone concerned will be free of this nightmare and can get on with their lives.

Keep sending the stalker aspect positive energy forms until you can feel that sense of release, relief and empowerment there too.

Finally, consider the relationship now. It will have changed considerably from when you first started.

What does this relationship need to evolve now completely so it resolves and frees both parties to go on to their highest possible outcomes in this lifetime?

Sometimes you find there's nothing that needs to be done after evolving the aspects involved, yours and theirs; sometimes it needs just a little something extra, because as soon as you put two together in the energy worlds, you get a system that is more than the sum of its parts.

I appreciate that just reading this may seem to be an overly simplistic approach to a very difficult problem, but if you have or ever had a stalker problem, try it for yourself.

Try it out and find out what happens when you apply that basic rule of the universe that in order to solve problems, you need more love, not less.

It's a fascinating experience when you start to feel the truth of the words of the prophets in your own body, and experience the blessings this brings in your own practical reality.

The X-Factor

When you know that the mysterious X-Factor is actually the state of our energy systems, the whole world starts making so much more sense, and a wonderful range of opportunities begin to exist that simply weren't there before.

- **A shiny energy system is attractive, and it's as simple as that.**

In modern energism, we don't work with pre-set charts and diagrams of thousands of nadis, or millions of acupuncture points that are here, there and everywhere.

We also essentially do not work with experts who are telling us what's wrong with us.

We are adults in charge of our own energy systems, and we can do with them as we please.

Every person's energy body is entirely unique and no map of it has ever been drawn.

I don't think you even can begin to draw a map of a shifting, multidimensional system that is so reactive, constantly in flow and in connection with the entire environment at all times ... and of course, with all the other energy systems in the vicinity ... and beyond that, as energy systems aren't as bound by time and space as our physical bodies are.

I am endlessly fascinated by these amazing energy systems we all have, and of which we know so very little.

That's only because we haven't paid attention enough; we can feel our energy systems just fine, and we can certainly notice what part they play in our lives.

This being so, I love simply tapping up the X-Factor.

We have healing hands of energy which touch our energy bodies when we do EFT, and all the conscious mind has to do is to hold attention.

Our energy bodies know absolutely what their problems are, and 99.999% of the time, the conscious mind really doesn't have the first clue or conception of what is wrong, where, or what to do to fix it.

When we tap to improve our X-Factor, we literally let the energy body sort it out.

The interesting thing is that we can't really predict what happens to our lives and our loves when we become more shiny, attractive, beautiful and lovable behind the material facade, whatever that might be.

We might guess based on old things, but those old things never factored in the reality of energy, so almost all of that previous experience and the conclusions we drew from it are probably way off the mark.

Whatever fears past aspects might have had about becoming more attractive, or stepping into their natural attractiveness and shinyness are irrelevant now, and that is always important to note.

We turn to the future and allow ourselves to be pleasantly surprised.

So, and to end this introduction to treating love problems with love via Positive EFT, let us - you and me both! - simply tap for our true and heartfelt desire to improve our X-Factor.

Let the healing ripple where it may, without frontiers, without reservations, and let the power of love uplift us, become our guide and goal, our method of the transformation and healing we have sought for so long.

Are you ready ...?

Put your hands on your heart and take three deep breaths.

I want to increase my X-Factor

With all my heart, I want to empower my energy system.

I want to increase my X-Factor, powerfully, now.

My powerful energy system is my birthright - increase my X-Factor!

All of nature wants me to increase my X-Factor!

I want to increase my X-Factor NOW - across the board and in every way!

Every day, my energy system grows stronger
and stronger - increase my X-Factor!

Increase my magical X-Factor! It's pure energy magic!

Increase my X-Factor so I feel and see more, experience more, live more!

Increase my bright and shiny X-Factor!

I release the shields that keep my shine inside - let me shine!

I want to shine as brightly as the sun, as the star I am. I am the star!

I am the star and I bring love and light.

Love and light.

Love and light.

Love and light.

186

In Conclusion: Make Love Your Goal!

As a modern energist, the power of love isn't just a phrase to me.

It is a structural reality, highly logical, and proven to be true, time and time afresh.

The heart centre is the nuclear reactor at the very core of our energy system. It powers everything else, and when the heart is broken, nothing in life can work.

Life becomes unbearably hard and we suffer from terrible stress manifestations in mind, body and spirit.

Now we have been working with positive energy forms since 2003, and you could sum that up by "love heals everything."

Everything in the energy body, that would be, but oh! my! That would be a start ...

I saw a group of ladies not long ago who were wondering how to have more success in business. I've been with such groups many times before, but this time, it really stood out to me that business was a side effect, and that what they all really needed was to be more loved.

Some had their hearts broken by previous relationships and were always angry below the surface; some were cold and stuck. Some were battling with having no support, no-one to have their back, to encourage them and cheer them on. All of them were full of all sorts of old entrainments about how you're not worthy of love; some were fat, some were old, some thought themselves ugly, and some all of that and then some.

All these ladies needed love to stand up in front of their customers and shine; they needed love so they could get up in the mornings and jump to work, write brilliant advertisements, and absolutely have love to give to their products, services and their customers.

Theoretically, the answer is stunningly simple. Put more energy through your system, get your energy system to run HIGHER and FASTER, more alive and then what happens?

You become instantly stronger, more confident, more capable and most importantly, you become far more ATTRACTIVE to other people!

All the negative self judgements simply disappear as our energy levels rise and we literally grow into our true selves, rise into our true selves, from the energy body out.

That's the power of love.

This beauty that shines from within, this X factor, totally transcends beauty, youth, intelligence, money - everything. It's the true form of attractiveness, and everyone, completely unconditionally, gets to own this when they start to empower their energy system.

We have all lived lives with way too little love for far too long. The problems we have with our relationships, with our health, with our finances, with any aspect of life whatsoever are all side effects of that one single common core problem - a lack of love.

For the first time in the history of humanity, we have a method to finally fix this. To fix this reliably, quickly, anywhere at all and just for the asking.

Positive EFT is the simplest method to not just get more energy into your life, but to expand your thinking, your mind, your understanding of the power inherent in such positives as love, romance, sex, joy, grace and bliss.

This is the reason that I am saying now, "This year, forget everything else. Forget your old troubles, your old woes, your pet problems and everything you think has held you back in the past.

"This time, do just one thing.

"**MAKE LOVE YOUR GOAL**."

I am absolutely convinced that I am right about this, but it would be wonderful to find out what happens to YOUR life if you gave that a go.

Make love your goal.

Let your heart of gold shine as brightly as the sun, ask, no, *demand* to experience more love in your life in every way, and every day.

To have the true miracle of love revealed to you, and then expanded into the infinity of love that is the very core of our Universe and all it holds.

Try it. And let me know what happened when you did!

Here's to an amazing future!

Silvia Hartmann

January 23rd, 2015

Index

philia: a strong feeling u love or
admiration & sth

Further Information

About The Author

Silvia Hartmann started researching the effects of energy exchanges and in particular, the effects of energy exchanges relating to aggression and attention seeking behaviour disorders, in the late 1980s.

In 1993, she formulated the original Harmony Program as the blue print for using attention and energy to cure emotional problems in social mammals. In 1996, Hartmann published Project Sanctuary, her breakthrough dissertation on energy, communication and metaphor relating to the energy mind (previously known as the sub- or unconscious mind).

In 1998, she came across EFT, found it fascinating and spent the next five years researching and experimenting with the Classic EFT protocol. From her findings, she created EmoTrance in 2002 as the first modern pure energy modality. In 2009, she published the SUE Scale and Events Psychology, the completion of the original Guiding Stars 2000 paper. In 2011, she designed Energy EFT and the new energist's trainings for The AMT (The Guild of Energists) and created Positive EFT as a training for working on the positive side of the SUE scale.

At present, Silvia Hartmann serves as the chair of The Guild of Energists, runs the GOE's Art & Creativity Group, as well as the Energist's Research Group and teaches the high level trainings in modern energism, bringing her unique perspective and visionary solutions to an ever growing international audience of leaders, teachers and trainers.

Find live courses & trainings at www.SilviaHartmann.com

Follow Silvia on Facebook: www.Facebook.com/theofficialsilviapage

Energy EFT from Beginner to Professional

Positive EFT by Silvia Hartmann

The bestselling introduction to modern Energy EFT and a great book for anyone to get started with EFT. Positive EFT is the breakthrough in powerful self help, and makes a great gift for a friend. Learn to overcome stress, dissolve emotional blocks and feel better - fast. With Positive EFT, you can't go wrong!

Energy EFT by Silvia Hartmann (Book & DVD)

The comprehensive guide for using modern Energy EFT to solve personal problems with many examples and a comprehensive A-Z of EFT, this outstanding book contains all the main patterns and techniques for those who want to go further with EFT. Required Reading for The AMT's EFT Master Practitioner Certification Program.

The EFT Master Practitioner Course (Manual & 12x DVDs)

For students of modern energy work, this is priceless information that is not available anywhere else in the world. Learn from Silvia Hartmann herself how modern Energy EFT works and take part in exciting exercises that will lead you to major shifts and demonstrate the power of EFT. Highly recommended for all counsellors, therapists, coaches and psychologists who wish to add Energy EFT to their modern practice.

The EFT Master Practitioner Certification Program (Live 3 Day Trainings or 12 Unit Distance Learning Option)

Learn the new patterns and techniques of modern Energy EFT and gain your certification as an AMT EFT Master Practitioner.

Other Books by Silvia Hartmann on Modern Energy

- **EMO Energy In Motion** - Modern energy without tapping - and without frontiers.
- **Events Psychology** - Finally understanding other people, and yourself!
- **Infinite Creativity** - Meet your energy mind ...

Courses by Silvia Hartmann on Modern Energy

- Positive EFT One Day Training
- Positive Energy One Day Training
- EFT Master Practitioner DVD Set - Available from www.DragonRising.com
- EFT Master Practitioner Training
- EMO Master Practitioner Training
- Project Sanctuary Masters Training
- The Master Energist Training
- The Modern Energist's Trainer's Training

**Live and Distance Learning Certification
courses at www.TheAMT.com/courses**

**Books available direct from www.DragonRising.com
and all good book shops, online and off.**

About The AMT - The Guild of Energists

Fascinated by modern energy work?

About The AMT - The Guild of Energists

The AMT is a not-for-profit learned society devoted to the study of energy work in all its forms. The AMT was founded in the United Kingdom in 1998 by Silvia Hartmann & Chrissie Hardisty and was one of the first organisations established in the world for the study of modern energy work including EFT Emotional Freedom Techniques.

Contact An AMT Practitioner

The AMT keeps a public register of professional energists who are qualified to help individuals and couples with modern energy techniques such as EFT, Energy EFT and Positive EFT. Each member adheres to the AMT code-of-conduct governing ethical practice.

Join The AMT

The AMT welcomes new members from all backgrounds who love energy. Anyone may join and we have membership options suitable for beginners, students, practitioners, trainers and retired professionals.

All members receive a number of benefits including the quarterly printed magazine "The Energist", premium member only downloads and access to a worldwide community of energists.

Experience The Joy & Power of EFT - Live!

AMT Trainers are conducting exciting day and introduction events, and professional trainings, all around the world. Learn EFT from the masters, practice in a safe space, have your questions answered and enjoy that special lifting of the group when energists get together.

The AMT Energy Conference

The best and brightest modern energy conference in the world is annually hosted by The AMT at the beautiful View Hotel in Eastbourne, UK. Learn the latest discoveries, state of the art techniques and spend time with other amazing people from around the world at the premier energy event of the year.

Further Information

Contact The AMT today by phoning **+44 (0)1323 700 800** (UK) or going online to:

- Main Website & Energy News: www.TheAMT.com
- About The AMT: www.TheAMT.com/about
- Practitioner Listing: www.TheAMT.com/practitioners
- Live Events, Distance Learning & Courses: www.TheAMT.com/courses
- Energy Conference: www.TheAMT.com/conference
- Join The AMT Today: www.TheAMT.com/join

Would you like to become qualified?

For licensed AMT training courses see:
www.TheAMT.com/courses

Just For Fun: Positive Energy Word Search

The Love Word Search is just a bit of fun, something to do and play with positives on a rainy day. You can try it with your partner to see what you both find, or notice which positives jump out at you today!

Look For Love :-)

```
E N E R G Y M A T A A E X P E C T A T I O N D N X
C I V Y S T R U T H L I G H T N E S S K Q B Q S Y
L A O T F U T R A N Q U I L L I T Y Z X H R I T B
A J A E G E C G A G B E A U T Y E P I H S E I R W
R R A G R C E C E A S Y B M Y C W R R A X S L E W
I S S P A R K L E H C L P E N E O A I C T P S N H
T E E A T E I M I S O B A E L T C M R E Y E L G T
Y N R S I A B H C N S V D R X O R S P M A C H T F
J S E S T T I O M Q G I U E X P N U T L T T A H U
L U N I U I N P Z H F O N M T R A G S A E H P N U
T A I O D V S E T N L O X P R I D N I T S T P V C
I L T N E I P T O O I M C A E D I C S N A Y I J O
M I Y C I T I C C T G Y E T A E E T T I G L N O N
E T E A X Y R S N L D S W H S A O A O S O B E R N
J Y S V U F A E W T T T L Y U T K B G M S N S A E
V I T A L I T Y E P D E S I R E A U E I U H S D C
S O U L K T I R A U R R N Q E Y W N T R N X H I T
C R S C A T O A L R B Y V D S C A D H A S E A A I
J E U A E L N D T P C S N Q E E R A E C H V R N O
C L L Z T X A Q H O N W E F J R E N R L I O M C N
E U A E D I C R E S O N A N C E N C N E N L O E C
R O I B B P S I H E T U U R D F E E E O E U N R V
T S L M L R O F T O P E N N E S S I S B R T Y B I
A V U A M E A T A E R L C F L L S D S S P I S R S
I P M P U O S T E C M B S Z I I T M I T A O W I I
N E A M P G R S I N T E O M G F I H L A T N O L O
T A G Z L O H T I O T I N Z H T L S O B I W N L N
Y C I Z A H R T A N N I O T T I L S V I E L D I E
T E C S Y M X T E L G P A N N N N P E L N Y E A G
E S C O A S A C Z R I S N L I G E A E I C D R N O
W T R A N S F O R M A T I O N V S C T T E K A C L
C S D B W I S D O M N Q Y J G I S E W Y Z H C E D
```

... and you will find it!